Collaborative
Leadership

Douglas Manion, for your continued support
and for always being there

Collaborative Leadership
Six Influences That Matter Most

Peter M. DeWitt

Foreword by John Hattie

Afterword by Russell Quaglia

A Joint Publication

FOR INFORMATION:

Corwin

A SAGE Company

2455 Teller Road

Thousand Oaks, California 91320

(800) 233-9936

www.corwin.com

SAGE Publications Ltd.

1 Oliver's Yard

55 City Road

London EC1Y 1SP

United Kingdom

SAGE Publications India Pvt. Ltd.

B 1/I 1 Mohan Cooperative Industrial Area

Mathura Road, New Delhi 110 044

India

SAGE Publications Asia-Pacific Pte. Ltd.

3 Church Street

#10-04 Samsung Hub

Singapore 049483

Printed in the United States of America.

Library of Congress Cataloging-in-Publication Data

Names: DeWitt, Peter M., author.

Title: Collaborative leadership : 6 influences that matter most / Peter M. DeWitt.

Description: Thousand Oaks, California : Corwin, a SAGE Company, 2016. | Includes bibliographical references and index.

Identifiers: LCCN 2016008170 | ISBN 978-1-5063-3711-1 (pbk. : alk. paper)

Subjects: LCSH: Educational leadership—United States. | School management and organization—United States. | Group work in education—United States.

Classification: LCC LB2805 .D48 2016 | DDC 371.2—dc23 LC record available at https://lccn.loc.gov/2016008170

This book is printed on acid-free paper.

Executive Editor: Arnis Burvikovs

Senior Associate Editor: Desirée A. Bartlett

Senior Editorial Assistant: Andrew Olson

Production Editor: Libby Larson

Copy Editor: Amy Harris

Typesetter: C&M Digitals (P) Ltd.

Proofreader: Sally Jaskold

Indexer: Joan Shapiro

Cover Designer: Michael Dubowe

Marketing Manager: Anna Marie Mesick

Certified Chain of Custody
SUSTAINABLE FORESTRY INITIATIVE
Promoting Sustainable Forestry
www.sfiprogram.org
SFI-01268
SFI label applies to text stock

19 20 21 10 9 8 7

Contents

Foreword

John Hattie

Models of leadership abound; it seems that any new model can be formed by simply inventing an adjective to preface the word *leadership*. Is "collaborative" leadership the new fad? It may well be if it takes all the old notions and merely repackages them under a slightly new hierarchy. It may well not be, if it distills an essence of "working together" with direction—but then we have had distributed leadership, transformational leadership, and so many more models that are based on working together. Peter DeWitt is quite specific about what he means—leaders need to be actively engaged in the learning process and enhance the instruction of all in the school to deepen learning for all (including their own learning).

Thus, "collaborative leadership" embodies the instructional focus, the deep and mastery notion, and the self-learning notion but centers on enhancing learning. The focus is not how we teach, who we teach, or what we teach but a balance between directing all to focus on enhancing learning. To know and maximize our impact! It begs the "impact" questions: "What do we mean by impact in this school, what is the desired impact we are aiming for in this school, and how many students gain this desired impact?" Impact should never be a neutral word but should be based on a collective understanding across the teachers (and also preferably across the students) about what it means to be "good at" something in this school. What are exemplars of a good grade five, of a good English assignment, of a good production for this student at this age or phase of their learning—and most importantly is this notion of impact a shared understanding? One of the greatest issues in our schools is that teachers so often do not share common conceptions of challenge, progress, or expectations. Thus, it can be random whether students thrive or stall depending on the conceptions of their teacher.

To share these conceptions requires excellent leadership. It requires building trust, it requires skill at conducting debates about shared notions of standards, it requires assembling multiple sources of evidence from teachers illustrating their notions of their expectations and standards, and it requires gentle pressure relentlessly pursued (as Michael Barber often claims). This notion of "collaboration" is the focus of this book.

In a recent meta-analysis, Rachel Eells (2011) found that teachers' collective efficacy has a very high relation to student achievement—across subject areas, when using varied instruments, and in multiple locations. Indeed, it is the new #1 of all the 200 influences I have investigated as part of Visible Learning (Hattie, 2009, 2012, 2015). Albert Bandura (1997) defined *collective efficacy* as "a group's shared belief in its conjoint capabilities to organize and execute the courses of action required producing given levels of attainments" (p. 477). Certainly, there is a cycle here, in that having higher collective efficacy needs to be supported by evidence of actually having an impact on student learning—which in turn fosters teachers' personal sense of efficacy, their professional practices, and their collective beliefs with their colleagues that they can actually make a major difference (Goddard, Hoy, & Woolfolk Hoy, 2004). There needs to be a sense of shared agency to make this difference, an agreement with group goal attainment, and a high level of trust among colleagues.

Note, the key is "teachers'" collective efficacy, thus a major role of school leaders is to keep a focus on this. How do we make transparent the collective notions of expectations, and as critical, how do we feed in the evidence of the impact of these expectations to further continue the cycle of showing that these expectations can be realized? The leadership role does not stop at building beliefs; they must then be enacted and fed back into the cycle, and there needs to be between-school triangulation that the local set of expectations are high and realizable.

Christine M. Rubie-Davies et al. (2012) have documented that teachers who hold high expectations typically do so for all students, and those who hold low expectations typically do so for all students—and both are successful in their respective ways. The high-expectation teachers have larger impact, the low kept their students low. She has investigated the classrooms of these teachers, followed them through the school year, and amassed a powerful defense of the importance of high expectations. It is likely to be no different for school leaders in their leading the narrative among their teachers about collective efficacy.

But there are many other aspects of leadership that must be present to ensure that the focus is on the collective impact of all adults in the school on the depth and mastery of their students. This is the strength of this book: the six influences that matter.

In this book, Peter DeWitt speaks of "flipped" leadership—which to me is akin to being clear about "success criteria"—making these transparent, making these criteria about learning, and making these shared. It means starting where the teachers are in their thinking, striving for continuous improvement, and then focusing on how to do it (see "The Cycle of Collaborative Leadership" figure in Chapter 5, p. 111). It involves "meet, model, and motivate," developing student assessment capabilities so that they too are part of this debate (and know how to interpret their own progress).

But "flipping" is not enough; there then needs to be a sustained concentration on seeking the evidence of the impact of the adults in the school. Not in any one way or overusing test scores or effect sizes (although they are part of the equation), but in many ways—privileging student voice about their learning, using artifacts of student work to show progress, and most of all, hearing how teachers share their thinking about where they are now, how they are going, and where they are going next. It involves clarity about diagnoses of where students are in their learning cycles, having multiple interventions to move them from where they are to where we want them to be, and continually evaluating the efficiency and effectiveness of these interventions. To use an acronym, teachers are to DIE for (Diagnoses, Interventions, and Evaluate).

But we add Peter's notion that the core business is learning—and this applies to the teachers and school leaders as much as for the students and parents. We know from an enormous research base that the most powerful impact of parents is their encouragement and expectations for their children (much more than financial resources, socioeconomic status, and parental involvement in schools). Thus, leaders have work to do with their teachers to show parents their own high expectations and have parents share, support, and realize these expectations. It is thus no surprise that there is a chapter on feedback and how to ensure that it is not only given appropriately and in a timely manner, but that we concentrate on how our feedback is received by teachers, students, and parents—and of course received by leaders about their impact. Developing and maintaining high expectations and the ability and willingness to receive feedback are core tasks for successful leaders.

Underlying this model of collaborative leadership is the building of trust. Trust can be considered the willingness to be vulnerable to another party based on the confidence that the other part is benevolent, honest, open, reliable, and competent (Tschannen-Moran & Gareis, 2015). Such trust is often a victim of high stakes accountability, not present when a principal focuses on "outside school" issues and whenever the politics of distraction are the narratives within and across schools (Hattie, 2015). Megan Tschannen-Moran and Christopher Gareis also noted that when the adults in a school trust one another, they are more likely to extend trust to their students as well; but distrust breeds more distrust. The development of trust starts with caring or benevolence, leading to a genuine care for the development of learning. School leaders thence win the trust of their teams through their willingness to extend trust, "which is evidence through openness, influence over organizational decisions, and professional discretion. Teachers see principals as trustworthy when their communication is both accurate and forthcoming" (p. 261). When a high level of trust prevails, a sense of collective efficacy follows.

The school needs to be safe and fair to welcome each teacher's beliefs and expectations. It is worth noting that this trust is fundamental also to the therapeutic process. In this literature it is often called the client–therapist alliance (Bachelor, 2013), and we could rephrase it as the leader–teacher–student–parent alliance. One of the more consistent findings in the therapy literature is the low association between clients' and therapists' perceptions, showing important differences between the therapist and clients' views of the alliance. It is converting perception of the trust in the relation that is key to positive outcomes. This convergence is across many dimensions: the collaborative relationship, the productiveness of the work, an active commitment to their high expectations agreed in the school, the trust bond, and confidence in the learning and teaching process. Trust underpins the collaborative behavior necessary for cultivating high performance.

Peter is a friend and colleague; he is among the many who successfully implement the Visible Learning model in schools (Hattie, Masters, & Birch, 2015). He has written on flipped leadership and safe schools, has been a principal, and is among the best communicators (see his EdWeek blogs for evidence of this). These traits are present on every page—enjoy.

REFERENCES

Bachelor, A. (2013). Clients' and therapists' views of the therapeutic alliance: Similarities, differences and relationship to therapy outcome. *Clinical Psychology and Psychotherapy, 20*, 118–135.

Bandura, A. (1997). *Self-efficacy: The exercise of control*. New York, NY: Freeman.

Eells, R. (2011). *Meta-analysis of the relationship between collective teacher efficacy and student achievement* (Doctoral dissertation). *Dissertations, Paper 133*. http://ecommons.luc.edu/luc_diss/133

Goddard, R. D., Hoy, W. K., & Woolfolk Hoy, A. (2004). Collective efficacy beliefs: Theoretical developments, empirical evidence, and future directions. *Educational Researcher, 33*(3), 3–13.

Hattie, J. A. C. (2009). *Visible learning: A synthesis of 800+ meta-analyses on achievement.* Oxford, England: Routledge.

Hattie, J. A. C. (2012). *Visible learning for teachers. Maximizing impact on achievement.* Oxford, England: Routledge.

Hattie, J. A. C. (2015). The applicability of visible learning to higher education. *Scholarship of Teaching and Learning in Psychology, 1*(1), 79–91.

Hattie, J. A. C., Masters, D., & Birch, K. (2015). *Visible learning into action.* Abingdon, Oxon, England: Routledge.

Rubie-Davies, C. M., Flint, A., & McDonald, L. G. (2012). Teacher beliefs, teacher characteristics, and school contextual factors: What are the relationships? *British Journal of Educational Psychology, 82*(2), 270–288. doi:10.1111/j.2044-8279.2011.02025.x

Tschannen-Moran, M., & Gareis, C. R. (2015). Principals, trust and cultivating vibrant schools. *Societies, 5,* 256–276.

Preface

Do you remember life as a classroom teacher? As classroom teachers, we had a tendency to think everyone taught like we did. We assumed that everyone had discussions with students and established cooperative learning groups. We also assumed that everyone treated students with a great deal of respect and helped foster student voice. Not that we couldn't improve on our practice, because we always could, but we thought that all teachers reflected and researched innovative ideas like we did. Then we became building leaders and realized that not all teachers were the same. Some needed a great deal of growth while others were our high flyers who we learned a great deal from every time we walked into their classrooms.

The same can be said for when our perspective changed to realize that not all leaders led their buildings or districts the same. As an author and consultant, my perspective has changed greatly when it comes to leadership, much the same as it did when I took on the building role from being in the classroom. Not all leaders are the same, but regardless of whether they have large areas of growth or are high flyers, they need help "moving their dial," which means they need help moving beyond their own expectations.

That's why I wrote this book. It is written for every leader who wants to collaborate more effectively around influences that matter and provide impact for student learning. Over the last year, I have reflected on how I led a school and have had the luxury of learning from great leaders around North America and internationally, all of whom have helped expand my thinking about leadership. Besides the practical and innovative ideas that I picked up, I have been profoundly impacted by working with John Hattie, Jim Knight, and Russ Quaglia. Their advice, innovative research, and ideas have all influenced me over the year I have taken to write this book. I went from focusing on instructional leadership to realizing there is so much more needed than just being good with instructional practices and that's when I decided to focus on collaboration. I know what you may be thinking: Do we really need a new type of leadership?

Collaborative Leadership

What's wrong with instructional or transformational leadership? Collaborative leadership is preferable to transformational and instructional leadership because it is more comprehensive and holistic in that it incorporates both transformational leadership and instructional leadership, as well as other tenets of good leadership while also ensuring that all stakeholders are included as active participants and ensuring that collaborative objectives are carried out. We have seen far too many initiatives and innovative ideas fail because parents and students had no idea what was going on in the school. Collaborative leaders find a balance between leading initiatives and fostering cooperative learning between adults with diverse ideas. And they have to do it during the good times that seem like each day is easy, as well as the tough times when it seems like they're faced with one more mandate every day. Collaborative leaders are responsible for inspiring and modeling learning, but they must also make sure that the co-constructed objectives they set out to accomplish have the support and understanding of the various stakeholders involved, whether that be parents, teachers, other district officials, or relevant community members.

Why collaborative leadership? Because it is more inclusive of all parties and therefore more effective in the long run. Collaborative leadership has as an objective finding the most informed, most capable person or persons to lead the charge.

At the same time, the leader is effectively communicating changes to parties who can't be involved at the time; not every stakeholder has the time, opportunity, or ability to be involved each time a new initiative is implemented. Sometimes the best leader for a specific job is not the titular leader; sometimes it is a fellow administrator, teacher, staff member, parent, or, in some cases, a student.

WHAT YOU WILL FIND IN THIS BOOK

This book draws on my experiences as a teacher and principal, as well as my experience working with John Hattie over the last two years. Hattie has the largest research base of any researcher in the world of education, and I have learned a lot from him. However, I also understand, from my experiences of providing professional development on the road, that leaders are looking for starting points, which I also provide in this book. Additionally, it brings together a great deal of practical advice from leaders at the elementary, middle, and high school levels from all around North America.

WHY THIS BOOK?

This book is different because

- it focuses on collaborative leadership and explains why collaborative leadership (either on its own or in conjunction with transformation and instructional leadership) is preferable to other types of leadership in isolation.
- it highlights six of John Hattie's influences that foster collaborative leadership so that leaders can place a laser-like focus on these few influences rather than being overwhelmed by the many.
- it draws on the excellent work and research of great educational thinkers such as Hattie, Quaglia, and Knight.

- it helps leaders understand why some teachers may not be as invested as they could be and the research behind collective teacher efficacy to get those teachers more engaged.

After you read this book, you will be able to

- transform your leadership practice into one that is more collaborative, research based, and effective.
- understand where you can start making changes that will help foster growth in students and teachers. Each chapter focuses on a different influence researched by Hattie.
- build a leadership team that relies more on each member and the team as a whole rather than looking to you as the primary leader.
- provide more stakeholders with a voice in the school community. This doesn't mean they will always get what they want, but it does mean they will feel welcome and heard as active participants.
- empower key members of your staff to be part of a collaborative leadership team.
- draw a variety of stakeholders into your leadership plan and activities including teachers, parents, and community members.

Acknowledgments

Book-writing may seem like a solitary pursuit, but very few writers ever do it alone. It is a collaborative effort. Besides my partner Doug, I never would have made it through life without my mom, as well as my siblings, Trish Choukeir, Frank DeWitt, Jody DeWitt, Dawn DeWitt, and all my nephews and nieces.

Thanks to my friends Jill Berkowicz, Linda Kindlon, Laurie Sweet, Jenni Donohoo, Beth Justiniano, and Randy Stevens.

To everyone from my Corwin family—Kristin Anderson offered me this amazing ride, and Mayan McDermott, Emily Malatesta, Mike Soules, and Lisa Shaw have supported me every step of the way.

To my professional/personal learning network (PLN), which includes Patti Siano, Lisa Meade, Vicki Day, Christina Luce, Tim Dawkins, John Harper, Kris Mitzner, and Michelle Hebert.

To Sarah Johnson, Mark French, Leah Whitford, Adam Welcome, and Cathy Worley for lending their voices for school stories.

To the QISA Team—Mickey Corso, Kris Fox, Brian Connelly, Ray McNulty, Susan Inman, Sue Harper, Lisa Lande, and Deb Young.

To Kathleen Manzo and Elizabeth Rich at *Education Week*.

To the students, staff, and parents at Poestenkill Elementary School—thank you for helping me grow as a leader.

I have been fortunate enough to work, learn, and become friends with Deb Masters, Helen Butler, Jennifer Sesta, and

Jayne-Ann Young. As well, John Hattie, Jim Knight, and Russ Quaglia have taken me on, become friends, and helped me grow as a learner, writer, and presenter.

And last but not least, thanks to Arnis Burvikovs, Ariel Bartlett, Desirée Bartlett, and Andrew Olson. They have supported my growth as a writer over the years and I love working with this team.

CORWIN GRATEFULLY ACKNOWLEDGES THE CONTRIBUTIONS OF THE FOLLOWING REVIEWERS:

Sara Armstrong
Educational Consultant
Sara Armstrong Consulting
Berkeley, CA

Jill Berkowicz
Professor, Author, Educational Consultant
SUNY New Paltz, Corwin Author
New Paltz, NY

Michael J. Corso
Chief Academic Officer
Quaglia Institute for Student Aspirations
Portland, ME

Kristine Fox
Senior Field Specialist
Quaglia Institute for Student Aspirations
Portland, ME

Lyman Goding
Senior Instructor
Secondary Education and Professional Programs
Bridgewater State University, MA

Louis Lim
Vice-Principal
Bayview Secondary School
Richmond Hill, Ontario, Canada

Dave Nagel
Consultant and Author, Effective Grading
    Practices for Secondary Teachers
Founder – NZJ Learning
Zionsville, IN

Moss Pike
Latin Teacher
Harvard-Westlake School
Los Angeles, CA

Dana Salles Trevethan
Interim Superintendent
Turlock Unified School District
Turlock, CA

Janice Wyatt-Ross
Interim Associate Principal
Bryan Station High School
Lexington, KY

About the Author

 **Peter M. DeWitt (EdD)** taught for eleven years and was a school principal for eight years. He runs workshops and provides keynotes focusing on collaborative leadership, fostering inclusive school climates, and connected learning.

Peter is a Visible Learning Trainer for John Hattie, Instructional Coach for Jim Knight, and Student Voice Advocate for Russ Quaglia working nationally and internationally. He is the series editor for the *Connected Educator* Series (Corwin) and the forthcoming *Impact Leadership* Series (Corwin).

His *Finding Common Ground* blog is published by *Education Week* and he is a freelance writer for *Vanguard* magazine (SAANYS). He is the 2013 School Administrators Association of New York State's (SAANYS) Outstanding Educator of the Year, and the 2015 Bammy Award winner for Education Blogger of the Year (Academy of Education Arts & Sciences).

Peter's first educational book, *Dignity for All: Safeguarding LGBT Students*, was published in 2012 and was the topic of his doctoral dissertation. In 2013, Peter contributed a chapter to *De-Testing and De-Grading Schools: Authentic Alternatives to Accountability and Standardization* (Peter Lang, USA). His other books include *School Climate Change: How Do I Foster a Positive School Climate* (ASCD, 2014; coauthored with Sean Slade) and *Flipping Leadership Doesn't Mean Reinventing the Wheel* (Corwin, 2014). Peter is the co-chair of the National School Climate Council. His articles have appeared in education journals at the state, national, and international level. He has written for *Principal Magazine, Education Week, Educational Leadership, The Huffington Post,* PBS, ASCD Whole Child, *Connected Principals, SmartBlogs,* and *ASCD Express.*

Peter has presented at forums, conferences, and panel discussions at state, national, and international conferences. Some of the highlights have been to present for the National Association of Elementary School Principals (NAESP 2012, 2014, & 2015), the Association of Supervision and Curriculum Development (ASCD 2012, 2015, 2016), ICLE's Model Schools, and Osiris World Conference in London, and to sit on a School Safety panel on NBC's Education Nation with Goldie Hawn and Hoda Kotb.

Peter has worked with the American Association of School Administrators (AASA), the National Education Association (NEA), the National Association of Secondary School Principals (NASSP), the National Association of School Psychologists, the Association of Supervision and Curriculum Development (ASCD), the National School Climate Center, GLSEN, PBS, NBC, NPR, BAM Radio Network, and ABCnews.com.

1

What Do You Want to Be to Leadership?

The first test is knowing what you want, knowing your abilities and capacities, and recognizing the difference between the two.

Warren Bennis

WHAT IF YOU COULD BE THE KIND OF PRINCIPAL YOU WANT TO BE?

When I was a young teacher pursuing my master's degree in educational psychology, the principal where I taught advised that I should change majors and pursue a degree in school administration. Being young and the first in my family to go to college and become a teacher, a principalship seemed way beyond my future aspirations. "I never want to be a principal," was my polite, yet short, reply.

In my limited experience as a teacher, I believed that principals were like Darth Vader in *Star Wars* and even heard that going into administration was like going to the dark side. Principals did all of the discipline, were the ones good students avoided, held difficult parent meetings, and forced teachers to do things against their will. Pretty extreme thinking and very naive on my part.

Fortunately for me, I used to talk to Joe and Tony, two guys from the local gym in Poughkeepsie, New York, who were retired teachers, and their response when I told them about my principal's suggestion was, "What if you could be the kind of principal you want to be?" Although not at the time, those words changed my perspective in the years to come because they never left the back of my mind. Something about those words stuck with me. I still believe to this day that the principalship has a great deal of potential, and sadly, some leaders never truly tap into all of it. It's one of those positions that we can look back on when we are old and gray and be proud of the fact that we were a principal.

Later on, after pursuing an advanced degree in administration, I did get the opportunity to take that administration job that I never thought I wanted. The teachers on the seventeen-member interview panel told me that their decision to choose me was based on the fact that I had a great deal of teaching experience. However, even with all of that teaching experience, when Jo Moccia, my superintendent at the time, formally offered me the job, I was a bit nervous and insecure.

I was hired to replace the current principal, Sharon Lawrence, who had been hired as the new assistant superintendent. During the three-month transition period before Sharon and I would start our new jobs, she was very supportive and introduced me to all of the key stakeholders in the school and community. If Sharon hadn't been so open and welcomed me into the school, it would not have been a successful venture. We worked as a team and it turned out to be one of the smartest things we ever did.

MOTIVATING PEOPLE TO
BE THEIR BEST EVERY DAY

Even though I knew everyone by July 1, I still knew that was only a small part of the journey into the principalship. The first faculty meeting, which I was very anxious about, was supposed to last one hour and went on for three. I made mistakes, but my staff supported me because I was open to hearing their feedback. I spent the first year of my principalship watching how people interacted with one another. Meeting people where they were was important because I wanted to help them reach another level. Truth be told, I wanted to reach another level and wasn't always sure how to do it. Every morning, I welcomed students off the bus and went to every classroom to say good morning.

The instructional side of leadership and the need to collaborate with staff was a bit more difficult. I entered classrooms, only after I told teachers that I was doing it to get to know students and not to evaluate their every move. Over time, I began transitioning into being more of a collaborative leader. I honestly did it because I missed being in the classroom, had a profound respect for education, and wanted to motivate people to improve and be the best they could be every day. I wanted to model positive relationships but also learn from those teachers, parents, and students around me. During my years as a teacher, I have learned a great deal from my students. My students taught me a lot about overcoming obstacles and have helped inspire me to wonder why we do what we do.

Part of that wondering led me to realize that my style of leadership differed from a straightforward instructional leader. Instead, my style was much more collaborative in that our staff, students, and parents learned from me and I learned from them.

WHAT IS COLLABORATIVE LEADERSHIP?

Collaborative leadership includes the purposeful actions we take as leaders to enhance the instruction of teachers, build deep relationships with all stakeholders, and deepen our learning together. It includes the managerial side, as well as instructional and transformational leadership, and is the greater whole of all of those parts. Collaborative leaders co-construct classroom and building-level goals with staff around the teacher observation process and faculty meeting agendas, we include parents in the conversation about the way their children learn and, when appropriate, we include students in the decision-making as well. Collaborative leadership is about working in collaboration with all stakeholders, and not manipulating people to agree with the goals we have already chosen. We bring our own expertise and learn together.

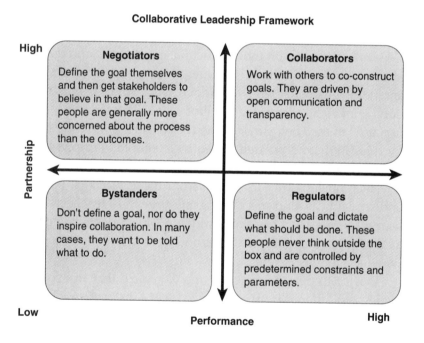

Collaborative Leadership Framework

For leaders to have a positive impact on relationships and learning, we need to establish a positive school climate and include all of the adults in the school in that collective endeavor.

There are four different ways to describe leadership styles with regard to collaboration proficiency:

1. **Bystanders**—These leaders don't define any positive goals and they don't inspire stakeholders to collaborate. They have low growth performance and low partnership qualities. Teachers work in silos and the principals remain in their office more than they make attempts to be visible.

2. **Regulators**—These leaders define the goals for the teachers and the school. Although they have high performance, they control the whole environment. These leaders know what idea they want to walk out of a meeting with well before they ever walk into the meeting. Unfortunately, they do not inspire true partnerships around the school as much as they promote compliance, which ultimately creates a hostile school climate where teachers wait to be told what to do.

3. **Negotiators**—Negotiators seem as though they are inspiring collaboration, but what they do is define the goal behind closed doors. Then they slowly make their way around the school or district and get people on board with their ideas. They create coalitions. This works just as long as stakeholders believe in the goal, rather than feel they have to achieve it because it's coming from the top.

> The Collaborative Leader finds the perfect balance between inspiring stakeholders and co-constructing goals

4. **Collaborators**—These leaders find the perfect balance between inspiring stakeholders to collaborate and co-constructing building- and classroom-level goals. They believe in a high level of transparency and honesty and have a high level of performance because stakeholders feel as though they have a voice in the process. Collaborative leaders use social media as one way to communicate with parents, and they utilize technology in ways that will maximize impact.

Hearing the words *collaborative leadership* should conjure up images of principals entering into classrooms, talking with students in the hallway, reaching out to parents to deliver positive messages about their children, and much, much more. Everything leaders do should be about having an impact, which means they have to work collaboratively with all stakeholders.

Having an impact means that we research, reflect, and have discussions around influences that matter. Influences refer to the tools and methods we use, as well as the actions we take in classrooms and school buildings that have a positive impact on learning. John Hattie, someone I will focus on a lot throughout the book, found over 150 influences on learning. Hattie's influences all have an effect size of over .40, which means that they offer more than a year's growth for a year's input, something I will further explain in the coming chapters.

> These influences were chosen based on how they work to collaboratively bring stakeholders together to foster growth through maximizing strengths and contributions.

The influences I chose for this book are based not only on their effect size but on how they work to collaboratively bring stakeholders together to foster growth through maximizing their strengths and contributions. These influences are

- Instructional Leadership (.42)—Being an instructional leader is specifically about putting a focus on learning; collaborative leaders bring stakeholders together in order to keep that focus.
- Collective Teacher Efficacy (1.57)—Each stakeholder in a school has a strength. This influence is about bringing those individuals together to maximize that strength with a goal of fostering a stronger focus on learning. Collaborative leaders foster collaborative expertise.
- Assessment-capable learning (1.44)—Hattie tells us it is important for all students to know where they are, how they got there, and where they should go to next. Collaborative leadership is needed to help build relationships with students, meet them where they are, and bring them to a new level.

- Professional development (.51)—Professional development is beneficial when it is ongoing and focuses on student learning, the goals of teachers, and the school community. Collaborative leaders foster and inspire professional learning and use their venues such as faculty meetings in order to do it.
- Feedback (.75)—Collaborative leaders foster growth in stakeholders and themselves, and feedback is what will help get them there.
- Family engagement (.49)—In order to have parental support, parents need to know what changes are happening in the school, and they need to feel as if they have a voice in some of the process. Collaborative leaders bring diverse parents together in order to meet this goal.

These are the influences that most leaders and school communities gravitate to when we provide Visible Learning trainings. Chapters 2 through 7 are each based on one of these influences. Take a moment to reflect on what helps you make an impact. Do you already use these influences? What kind of evidence do you have to prove that what you do works? How do you know you are having an impact? Which one of the influences that you haven't tried yet will be the one that helps you make a stronger impact?

Both you and the teachers at your school should be collecting evidence to understand your impact on student learning (collectively and individually). Your job as a collaborative leader is to figure out ways to help teachers understand what evidence to collect as well as how to find resources to help them improve their practices. If we are reflecting without evidence, then we are just remembering it the way we think it happened as opposed to how it may really have happened. Collaborative leadership is about bringing teachers together to discuss the evidence they have and figuring out ways to make a stronger impact on student learning so that students can become assessment-capable learners.

Collaborative leaders

- use evidence when reflecting,
- work proactively by fostering a positive school climate,
- take a breath before being reactive,
- listen more than they talk,
- bring people together through finding common bonds, and
- know why they chose to get into leadership and understand why they stay there.

MEET, MODEL, & MOTIVATE

A collaborative leader is someone who uses evidence and research to **meet** stakeholders where they are, **models** how to do it and **motivates** them to improve (see Figure 1). What makes collaborators different from negotiators is that while

Figure 1   Meet, Model, & Motivate

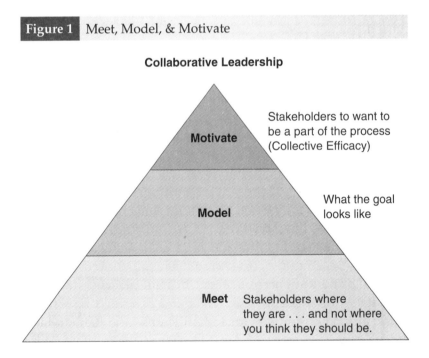

Collaborative Leadership

Motivate — Stakeholders to want to be a part of the process (Collective Efficacy)

Model — What the goal looks like

Meet — Stakeholders where they are . . . and not where you think they should be.

collaborators may bring their own ideas, they are open to changing these ideas based on the feedback of the stakeholders they are working with. Additionally, the reason why this framework needs to be highlighted is because I do not believe that a majority of leaders meet stakeholders where they are, but actually meet stakeholders where they, as leaders, think those stakeholders should be. Additionally, leaders do not motivate stakeholders as much as they use data to force those stakeholders into compliance. And they rarely model as much as they act as though stakeholders should "Do as I say and not as I do."

We need to ask ourselves who we are as leaders. What does leadership mean to us as individuals? What are we willing to learn? Are we in front of our staff or working side by side—or both? We are living and working during extraordinary times in education, which brings accountability in a magnitude that has not been present before. Many critical issues are facing us as leaders, and although some of them have been around for a few years, we still don't understand how to best deal with them. They are not going away any time soon, and we have to know what they are as well as how to address them. We need to work in collaboration with stakeholders to find the best way to address these large issues at the same time we work on the small ones.

10 CRITICAL ISSUES FACING EDUCATION

In January of 2014, I posted a blog titled *10 Critical Issues Facing Education*. It has had hundreds of thousands of views and continues to receive over 15,000 views a month, which shows that it still resonates today. These issues are still critical. Leaders are still trying to figure them out, and they will only address the issues, and do their best thinking around them, when they work in collaboration with stakeholders from their school community.

10 Critical Issues Facing Education

by Peter DeWitt

January 23, 2014

blogs.edweek.org

During my leadership training at the College of Saint Rose, I took a class with Jim Butterworth (my mentor) called Critical Issues. Jim was a voracious reader, an assistant commissioner for the New York State Education Department, former superintendent, and an amazing professor. All of those combined with a 2 ½ hour class led to some of the best educational discussions I've ever had.

Every week, we were required to read chapters from various books (i.e., Fullan, Senge, Hargreaves, Reeves and Greenleaf), and numerous stories from *Education Week*'s print copy. It opened up our world from the classroom we were teaching in, or the school we were leading. The class brought together building leaders, teachers, school psychologists, and social workers from urban, suburban and rural settings who were all trying to finish their degree in leadership.

I took the class over 10 years ago but never forgot about the importance of discussing issues, even if they were difficult and the people in the room held differing opinions. As educators, we should always be able to debate our profession. The problem we have, as does anything that involves politics, is that we cannot seem to move forward together. There are state and national leaders so consumed with being right that they cannot, and will not, budge.

Hopefully, all of that will change this year. After the past few years of increased accountability, budget cuts, arguments, and infighting, 2014 will be a different year for all of us . . . and I hope for the positive. In education, there are some very large issues that we have to contend with, and they are not all about accountability and mandates.

Top 10 Critical Issues

Critical issues are those issues that are important to education. They are the barriers that get in the way, or the important elements that we need to focus on in order to move forward and offer better opportunities to our students.

Common Core State Standards—Forty-six states may have adopted the standards but around a dozen states are backing out or considering backing out of using them. Regardless of how people feel about the Common Core, they have led to many hot debates about education and will continue to do so in 2014.

Student Learning—Student learning is everything from different pathways to graduation; encouraging student voice in student learning, and encouraging students to have a place at the table for larger conversations about their education. So often we focus on teaching, but it's learning that matters most.

Technology—Even after all of these years, technology is still a hot button issue. Some people love it and use it flawlessly every day, while others hate it and don't see why they need to be forced to use it at all. In addition, what makes it complicated is that some schools seem to have endless resources, while other schools have to use what wealthier schools disregarded as old. Whether its MOOCs, iPads, gaming, or BYOD, technology will still be a critical issue to discuss in 2014.

Social Media—Twitter has exploded over the past few years. More and more educators are joining and finding members to their professional learning network (PLN). What's even better is that they are sharing resources to use in their classrooms, buildings, and districts, and they are also using social media to connect for professional development (e.g., Twitter chats, EdCamps, etc.). Social media will be, and should be, part of a huge discussion in 2014.

Politics—Politicians have long mentioned education in their speeches but the past two years it seemed to have happened more than ever. Many politicians seem to focus on how schools are failing, and their only solution is standardization, accountability, and high stakes testing. Many governors are running for reelection this year and education will no doubt make or break their campaigns. How many politicians, like Cuomo and Christie, have spoken about teachers is deplorable and this is the year when teachers continue to take control over that conversation.

(Continued)

(Continued)

High Stakes Testing—Not sure if you have heard of this before but schools across the country have to give high stakes tests to students. Some start it in kindergarten, while others begin in 3rd grade. In most states, they are tied to teacher/administrator evaluation and that will no doubt continue to be a big debate this year. There need to be different methods used to assess student learning, and none of it should be "high stakes."

School Leadership—If you go on Twitter, you will find hundreds of school leaders who consider themselves "Lead Learners." This is very important because they see the important part they play in the lives of their students, teachers, and staff. In addition, school leaders understand that they can have a positive or negative impact on their school climate, and too many still have a negative impact.

Preservice Teaching Programs—How can we get the best teachers into our classrooms when so many politicians and policymakers cry that schools are failing? Under those circumstances, who would want to go into the profession? Additionally, preservice programs need to improve because many of the graduates do not seem prepared for the profession. The real question for 2014 is how can K–12 schools work with these programs to build a community of learners who are prepared for the profession? A little less accountability tied to testing would go a long way to improve this issue.

School Climate—A few days ago Secretary Duncan and Attorney General Eric Holder announced new guidelines to stop the school to prison pipeline and improve school climate. This critical issue is not just about bullying, but about creating an inclusive school climate where all students can achieve their maximum potential.

Poverty—We know around 22 percent of our students are living in poverty. We also know that many children who live in poverty come to kindergarten hearing one-eighth of the language (vocabulary) that their wealthier peers experienced. Many of the schools that try to educate these students lack the proper resources, and the communities where children in poverty live often lack the same resources that wealthier towns have. Poverty is an issue that is one of the most critical issues of our time, in and out of schools.

These are very tough issues, but also very exciting at the same time, and we need collaborative leaders who have a depth of knowledge about each one. Collaborative leaders are the ones who don't ignore the issues, but look at them as challenges. Our lives are always followed by question marks because we don't know what will happen, but part of the excitement is figuring out how to react to those question marks. Collaborative leaders rally their stakeholders to move forward in a way that will bring out the best thinking that can help alleviate the pain some of the issues may cause, something I will better address throughout this book.

The Importance of Reflection

I'm forever grateful for my time as a school leader. Reflection has been a vital element for my career, and I still think a great deal of growth lies before me. Hopefully you feel the same way about your own leadership practices. I hope this book inspires you and provides you with the tools you need to reflect with evidence in your own practice.

Jill Berkowicz, a former teacher who writes the *Leadership 360* blog (Education Week) with Ann Myers, posed these questions that I will leave for you to answer as you begin to read this book:

- Who are you?
- Who do you want to be to the educational field?
- What do you know and can teach that is different from the masses?
- How will your voice speak to a need in the field?
- What will you do if you have hesitations about standing out as yourself?
- How will you know you are ready?

Answering these questions will undoubtedly help you lead your classroom, school, or district. In order to lead effectively and positively impact our school communities, we need to find our voices and stand out as leaders who invite collaboration rather than compliance

In order for things to change for the better, school stake-holders need strong collaborative leaders who will encourage them to have a voice in their school community. Are you an empowering leader?

Collaborative leadership is far from easy because it involves bringing different mind-sets together under one common mission and takes a great deal of experience, patience, and a bit of foresight. In administration classes, prospective leaders are told to be visible, and I believe we need more than that. Leaders need to go deeper every day. They need to meet, model, and motivate. That doesn't happen overnight and takes time to evolve.

///

School Story—Many Hands Make Light Work

by Peter DeWitt, Principal of
Poestenkill Elementary School

Albany, NY

As the principal of Poestenkill Elementary School in the Averill Park Central School District outside of Albany, New York, I worked hard to collaborate with parents, students, and staff. Although there will be school stories throughout this book, I wanted to start with mine because it has elements that were both highly successful and very challenging.

Most days involved me taking students off the bus, checking in with the students who needed some sensitive adult intervention, and going from one classroom to the next to say good morning to all of the students as they started their day. School climate was important to me and the staff, and we wanted to try our best to start each day off right. Sometimes that meant working through an issue with a parent, listening to the concerns of teachers and staff, or getting feedback from students.

As a school community, we collaborated by designing and building a playground together. Dozens and dozens of parents, as well as teachers and students, came together over multiple weekends to build a playground for the school community. This was a big deal because the small town didn't really have any other large areas where children could play, so the school played a central role in the town. One of the parents kept rallying our energy by stating, "Many hands make light work." It was a really great time for our school climate and school community. Staff, students, and parents always felt comfortable sharing concerns and celebrating successes, but the playground construction really helped us strengthen our foundation. Those first few years were important for what was to come.

In the last four years of my principalship, our school community went through millions of dollars in budget cuts, numerous teacher lay-offs, and a school consolidation based on low enrollment that required us to close a one-classroom-per-grade-level school that had been annexed into the school district in 1992. Poestenkill Elementary School had to absorb the whole student population within about three months, as well as some of the teachers from the school that was being closed.

It was a tumultuous time in our district because second graders were picketing at board meetings, parents from both schools were arguing through Facebook, and a parent from the school that was closing created a hate blog that focused on school administrators and teachers. There were times when the state police had to be at board of education meetings. During the consolidation, we all made mistakes that we had to learn from, which usually centered on communication.

In my first year as the principal, we had established a Principals Advisory Council (PAC) in our school. PAC required one stakeholder from each grade level and special area to voluntarily sit on the committee. Over the time we were together, we began co-constructing goals for faculty meetings and addressed building issues through activities that would draw out where we needed to focus. During the time of the consolidation, we spent a lot of time focusing on how to lessen the stress of all stakeholders.

- We created an open house for the parents of the school we consolidated.
- I visited the students at the school several times before it closed, and a couple of those visits were during the whole school assemblies.

- We developed an ice cream social with our PTA to bring all of our students together before school officially started.
- When the hate blog posted negative comments, we tried to combat it with positive responses around school.

> Collaboration is what helped me become a better leader. I learned from the students, teachers, and parents. Being the principal of Poestenkill Elementary will always be one of my proudest accomplishments.

Additionally, I worked with the PTA to create new events that would bring together the students and parents of both communities, and over time, the pain of the consolidation subsided. Parents, students, and teachers came together many times for plays, concerts, athletic events, and academic events as well. We had open houses that focused on having deep discussions on bullying and new state standards, all of which I will highlight throughout this book.

Collaboration isn't just a good idea for a book. Collaboration is what helped me become a better leader because I learned from the students, teachers, and parents around me. Being the principal of Poestenkill Elementary School will always be one of my proudest accomplishments.

Peter DeWitt, EdD

Principal, Poestenkill Elementary School (2006–2013)

Poestenkill, NY

MEET, MODEL, & MOTIVATE

Meet

- Introduce yourself to the school community. Let down any walls you may have and show them that you are honored to be working there. Parents want to know that their child's leader wants to be with them.

- Take time to get to know stakeholders one conversation at a time (students, teachers, etc.) to see where they are and begin thinking about ways you can offer your expertise.
- Listen more than you talk. Don't just spread your message. Learn what their message is as well.

Model

- Use good communication skills. Make sure your school website has the word *learning* on it.
- Try using one-page newsletters to send home instead of five-page newsletters that stakeholders may not read.
- Create a blog for your school so you can write about learning, and even about changes you have made to the school community. A blog will help you find your voice and model collaborative leadership as long as you do not shut down the comment section of the blog.
- Make sure you use positive words when talking about students, teachers, and school. It may sound silly to offer this advice, but we hear one positive statement for every ten negative statements.

Motivate

- Depending on the school community, many people have heard the typical rhetoric about high expectations and a sense of community. How will you offer a deeper narrative?
- Following through with your narrative is the biggest way to prove that you are serious. Leaders do not always follow through with their narrative. Choose the right one so you are more motivated to achieve it.
- Leaders talk about change. Be different and talk about improving. We are asked to change all the time, but improvement is where we should get the biggest bang for our bucks.
- How will you motivate the unmotivated? How do you know who they are? What will you do?

DISCUSSION QUESTIONS

- How did you begin your career as an administrator?
- How do you plan on meeting with stakeholders in the school community?
- Who can you go to for support and guidance? Your predecessor? A veteran teacher leader? A community member?
- What lessons from the classroom did you learn that can be used to help guide teachers who may go through the same thing?
- How will you focus on instruction and learning as a leader?

2

Instructional Leadership (.42)

The role of the leader is not to come up with all the great ideas. The role of the leader is to create an environment in which great ideas happen.

Simon Sinek

WHAT DO INSTRUCTIONAL LEADERS DO?

In the Preface, I wrote about how collaborative leadership combines a few different leadership styles. The first influence I would like to focus on is that of instructional leadership. As instructional leaders, we take actionable steps to improve the learning climate in our schools, but these steps must be based in research, and not just on gut feelings. Classroom visits, which are some of the best actionable steps we can take, help motivate teachers and principals to work together because the result is a clearer understanding of the classroom climate, teacher instructional practices, and student learning needs. Perhaps those visits through using coteaching a time or two will show students the power of the relationship between both teachers and administrators and demonstrate to students that the staff as a whole is committed to improving student learning by working together.

According to John Hattie (2009), school leaders have an effect size of .39 which is right under the hinge point of .40. Remember that the .40 hinge point means that there is an impact of at least a year's growth with a year's input. The larger the effect size the larger the impact on growth. Although school leadership is only .01 away, it's still an issue that it is less effective. We want a higher effect size for our leaders.

When looking at the moderators within Hattie's vast research, there are two types of leadership that come into focus. One is transformational leadership, which has an effect size of .11. That surprises many people. Transformational leadership has been a main focus in educational administration leadership courses for a long time. Transformational leadership is about shifting mind-sets and bringing teachers, parents, and students to another level. The point I want to make here is that once a school community is transformed, it needs to be led by an instructional leader.

Instructional leadership has an effect of .42, which is much higher than transformational leadership's effect size. In *Visible Learning for Teachers*, Hattie (2012a) writes,

> Instructional leaders attend to the quality and impact of all in the school on student learning, ensure that disruption to learning is minimized, have high expectations of teachers for their students, visit classrooms, and are concerned with interpreting evidence about the quality and nature of learning in the school. (p. 174)

Regarding instructional leadership, Hattie continues,

> The effects (according to Robinson, Lloyd, and Rowe, 2008) were strongest on promoting and participating

in teacher learning and development (.84), establishing goals and expectations (.42), planning, coordinating, and evaluating teaching and the curriculum (.42), aligning resource selection and allocation to priority teaching goals (.31), and then ensuring an orderly and supportive environment (.27). (p. 175)

As a school leader, I wanted to spend time in classrooms for a number of reasons. First and foremost is that I loved the magic of a classroom climate and wanted to spend time in each classroom to get an understanding of how teachers met the social and academic needs of students. Secondly, getting into classrooms afforded me the opportunity to create relationships with students.

Instructional leaders focus conversations around the learning that is happening in class. It includes asking questions such as "What are you learning today?" and "Why do you think you are learning it?" It also means we ask students what kind of feedback their teachers have provided to them, and get them to use common language like *feedback*.

> Instructional leaders focus conversations around the learning that is happening in class. It includes asking questions such as *"What are you learning today?"* and *"Why do you think you are learning it?"* It also means we ask students what kind of feedback their teachers have provided to them, and get them to use common language like *feedback*.

Instructional leaders also meet with staff to discuss what kind of learning dispositions, described by Hattie, are important, like resilience, grit, perseverance, and others. After staff decide on five or six learner dispositions, which moves us into collaborative leadership, it is time for staff to share those with students and parents, which then become common language across the school community.

Instructional leadership puts the focus on learning through the ways I just described, and collaborative leadership comes into play when we define the dispositions and communicate them to all stakeholders. Instructional leadership has an effect size of .42 which is great, but imagine how much higher the effect size will be when leaders become more collaborative.

We need to change our mind-sets from merely getting curriculum covered to thinking more about how we learn, why we learn, and how we can have a larger impact on student learning. That takes collaboration. Hattie finds collaboration to be so vital to learning that he created the tenth mindframe, "I collaborate." The following blog post illustrates the importance of these mindframes.

John Hattie's 10th Mindframe for Learning

October 20, 2015

by Peter DeWitt

blogs.edweek.org

We all teach, lead, and learn under different mindframes. They envelop our personal lives as well as our professional conversations. John Hattie, someone I have worked with for the last year and a half as a Visible Learning trainer, has written extensively about the nine mindframes our students need for learning. Those mindframes are equally as important for teachers and school leaders as well.

Hattie recently announced a tenth mindframe, which is easy to discuss but less easy to put into practice. First and foremost, Hattie believes that in order to maximize learning, we need to make sure that we embody the following nine mindframes:

- **I am an evaluator**—Evaluation isn't just about the formal evaluation that comes down from the state education department and district offices. As educators, we all have to evaluate whether our practices are bringing out the best learning in our students. After all, in Hattie's words, we have to "Know Thy Impact."
- **I am a change agent**—In these days of more accountability and more on the plates of teachers and leaders, it's easy to feel as though we are victims of our present educational situations. Hattie believes we have to change our mind-sets to understanding we are change agents. This is important because research

shows that when teachers have a low level of efficacy they feel as though they don't have any impact on student learning, which doesn't put them in the role of change agent at all. It's important for leaders to establish a school climate that fosters an increased sense of teacher efficacy so that they can build collective teacher efficacy as a staff and help teachers realize they may be one of the only change agents in a child's life.

- **I talk about learning and not about teaching**—When we talk about teaching, we are focusing on the adult in the room and very often forget about the students. The adult is important, but focusing on the student is more important. In the "Politics of Distraction," Hattie (2015a) wrote that school stakeholders, policy-makers, and politicians talk a great deal about the adult issues in school, such as unions, prep time, and teacher evaluation, but not enough time discussing learning.

- **I see assessment as feedback to me**—Ward et al. wrote that schools are awash with data but very often the data that we all have access to is not used at the depth that it could be because data has been used as a *gotcha* instead of a tool that could lead to deeper conversations. What sort of formative assessment (click here for this guest blog by Shirley Clarke) are we doing to make sure that what we are doing in the classroom is actually working?

- **I engage in dialogue and not monologue**—In these days of 24/7 communication tools, I wonder if we really listen to one another any better than we did before we had access to those tools? Do we engage in dialogue where we listen to the thoughts of the person on the other side of the conversation, or do we use the conversation to merely get our own self-interests across? In the classroom with students, do teachers listen to students or just lecture and talk at students without giving them enough time to debate and discuss?

- **I enjoy challenge**—Hattie believes we spend too much time giving students answers to questions that they struggle with in the classroom, instead of taking the opportunity to teach them that error is the best way to learn. It's through error that they dig deep within themselves. This will work better, if at a young age, we

(Continued)

(Continued)

teach students that learning is not always easy, which is one of the greatest parts of it.

- **I engage in positive relationships**—In Hattie's work, he has shown that teacher–student relationships have an effect size of .72, which is nearly double the hinge point (.40) he found through his research that offers a year's worth of growth for a year's input. Positive relationships, whether through teacher–student relationships or the relationships students have with peers, can have an enormous benefit.
- **I use the language of learning**—The focus on learning is important, which is why we need to talk about it more than we talk about teaching. However, having common language around learning is the crucial next step. Schools that focus on learner dispositions and teach students how and when to use them can help change the mind-set of school stakeholders.
- **I see learning as hard work**—All of the above mindframes come together in this mindframe. Engaging in dialogue, diving deeply into assessment data, teaching students about learning dispositions, and becoming change agents is no easy task, which is why learning is hard work.

The tenth mindframe that Hattie released last week is

- **I Collaborate**—Hattie not only has ten mindframes but within his research he found 150 influences on learning, which continues to grow. *I collaborate* is crucial to the influence that is near the top spot, which is collective teacher efficacy. We, as adults, teach students about the importance of collaboration, and team sports have hopefully been focusing on that issue as well. Unfortunately, adults still don't collaborate at grade levels and departments nearly as often as they should. It happens in pockets, but not always across schools.

In the End

The mindframes of learning serve an important role. Adults go to counselors and invest a great deal of time and energy into practices that will help them shift their mindframes at home. We need to do the same for our mindframes that we carry to work with us every day.

Collaboration which brings together diverse thinkers who engage in authentic conversation can help shift our thinking, which inspires us to grow as learners. It's why Twitter is so popular with educators because they find professional and personal learning networks, which help them think outside the box. Imagine how much better it would be if we didn't always have to go to social networking for that and could find it within our own buildings as well.

COLLABORATIVE LEADERSHIP: A POSITIVE EFFECT ON LEARNING

Hattie's research lends evidence to the fact that a collaborative mindframe is necessary to improve collective teacher efficacy. We also know that collaborative leaders can have a positive effect on student learning. Clearly, Hattie's research shows the more principals move into the role of instructional leadership—albeit creating dialogue around learning, a positive learning culture and climate, and focus on school aspirations that put focus learning at the center, which will have a positive impact on their schools—the more the research he collects for his meta-analysis will mirror that positive impact and the effect size will increase. In order to do that, leaders must collaborate effectively.

Based on the description of effect sizes, you might think that educators should only focus on influences with an effect size of .5 or higher. However, this would be a mistake. Consider class size. Hattie has long spoken about how class sizes haven't impacted student achievement because when teachers go from a large class to a smaller one, they hardly ever change their instruction. Therefore, according to the data, small class size doesn't have a high effect size. But if teachers changed their instruction in smaller classes, the data might well show that smaller classes resulted in a high effect size. Improving influences and effect sizes begins with constructive dialogue among teachers and leaders. This collaborative dialogue should ideally lead to a positive effect on learning.

A collaborative leader has to model the type of ongoing learning they wish to see in staff. Therefore, leaders need to provide staff with quality research that will inspire action at the same time it proves impact. As W. Edwards Deming once said, "Without data you're just another person with an opinion." We also need to seek out research that will motivate us to question our own long-held beliefs. Questioning beliefs is key to improving our impact. Students deserve the best teachers and leaders; therefore, we always need to be focused on improving how we teach and how we lead.

Hattie conducted decades of research around the world before he wrote the bestselling book *Visible Learning* (2009). He wanted to focus on what actually works in the classroom and get a better understanding of the impact teachers had, and still have, on student achievement. Additionally, he wanted to change the dialogue we have around schooling. It seemed to him that, whenever he asked teachers what worked best, they always had different answers, but they could not always support their opinions. And many times the conversations that teachers and leaders did have didn't focus on learning.

At the time he was writing the book, Hattie had collected over 800 meta-analyses of completed studies, both published and unpublished from developed countries around the world, on student achievement, which have now surpassed 1,100. These meta-analyses covered 139 influences, which have now become 150 and will continue to grow over time. Influences are any teaching strategies, school conditions, or home conditions that affect a student's performance, such as feedback, teacher–student relationships, project-based learning, open classrooms, class size, retention, homework, and so on. From the meta-analyses, Hattie determined one average effect size for each influence to show the impact that that influence would have on student learning.

He found that 95 percent of everything that teachers did had a positive effect on student achievement. The issue was that not all influences have a similar impact—some have a very small effect, some provide students with over a year's growth in a year's time, and many fall somewhere in between.

Through the research he conducted, Hattie found that the hinge point was where students achieved at least one year's progress after one year's input. The hinge point is a .40 effect size. There are influences that have a positive effect on learning (above .40 effect size) and others that have a negative effect on learning (below .40 effect size).

> Build dialogue with your staff that focuses on what works in the classroom and what does not, backed up with evidence. Teachers need to feel comfortable honestly sharing that kind of information, without feeling the need to be guarded because they may get "in trouble."

As a collaborative leader, it's important to build dialogue with staff that focuses on what works in the classroom and what does not; this is why evidence is important. We need evidence to support whether we are having an impact, and it takes collaborative leadership to dive deep into that discussion because teachers need to feel comfortable honestly sharing that kind of information, without feeling the need to be guarded because they may get "in trouble."

The blog post below shows how evidence can improve the collaborative effort of improving instruction and learning in schools.

Why We Need to Talk About Evidence

By Peter DeWitt

January 10, 2016

blogs.edweek.org

When it comes to data, I wasn't always on board. Data can sometimes be used to portray a story differently than it may be in reality, but my mind was changed after reading *Using Data to Focus Instructional Improvement* by

(Continued)

(Continued)

James-Ward, Fisher, Frey and Lapp (2013). In the book, the authors write, "Starting with the assumption that opportunities for improvement always exist, we must purposefully seek out errors, understand their causes and effects, and then fix them for continuous improvement to occur."

While I served as school principal, New York State required observations to be based in evidence. *I enjoyed observations. I enjoyed learning from teachers.* At its best, an observation should require teachers to meet with their school leader and define a common goal. Perhaps that goal is co-constructed between both parties or perhaps teachers are solely responsible for coming up with their own goal. Having an agreed upon goal provides the leader with something to look for during the observation. Feedback matters most when it's focused on a goal and not just given randomly.

When the leader and teacher meet up for the postobservation, they should both bring evidence to the meeting. The teachers should be able to explain their impact on student learning. We are responsible for "moving the dial" for the learners in front of us.

Data and evidence of late have been synonymous with test scores. But we all know there is a lot more to learning than test scores. For example, educational researchers and theorists such as Jim Knight, Carol Dweck, John Hattie, and Russ Quaglia have cited the following measures of learning:

Teacher talk versus student talk

Growth mind-set statements versus fixed mind-set statements

Negative interactions versus positive interactions

Cooperative learning versus cooperative seating

Surface-level versus deep-level questioning

Teachers and leaders working together can strategize ways to measure whether or not these evidences of learning are occurring in the classroom. They can also devise strategies to ensure that the desired behaviors continue to increase on an ongoing basis. This means finding ways to change the school environment to better serve the needs of the child. The collaborative leader has to do a lot of proactive work to create a safe and inclusive environment where these conversations can take place.

Challenge: At stakeholder meetings, you hear that "morale is low." How do you help change the collective mindframe to one that is more positive?

Suggestions: At your stakeholder meeting, provide chart paper and give three stickers to each member of the group.

- Have each member write all of the negatives issues that are affecting morale, even if that means using two pieces of chart paper.
- After members have written their issues, give them their three stickers and tell them they have to put one sticker next to their biggest issue or put all three stickers there if they like.
- After everyone puts their stickers on the chart, count which ones have the highest three votes and those will be the issues you work on at each stakeholder meeting.
- The group members are no longer the venters of bad morale and need to become the team that eradicates the highest issues—and those issues should all revolve around learning.

THE POLITICS THAT DISTRACT US FROM MAKING LEARNING THE MAIN PRIORITY

When we talk about school we seem to talk about adults a lot more than we talk about students. We do focus on teaching, instruction, unions, prep time, and common planning time a lot more than we seem to focus on learning and students. Hattie refers to this dilemma as the *politics of distraction.*

The politics of distraction that happens in schools means that too often we only focus on the adults in the school and talk about students as though they are products that we churn out from year to year. We slap a grade on their paper or label them with some sort of learning issue and put them through a conveyor belt of learning. In the world of high stakes testing, we put a number next to their name which follows them up from year to year, and we create a self-fulfilling prophecy that some of those students are "good at school" and others are not. Collaborative leaders expect more from their students, and they understand that we need to meet students where they are, motivate them to improve, and model what that love for learning may look like.

In the "Politics of Distraction" (2015a), Hattie writes,

> In my travels I have met with many political leaders and department officials and continue to be impressed with their commitment to improving their education systems, their desire to make them world-leading and their dedication to improving outcomes for students. (p. 1)

This may seem like a surprise from those of us who have had to put up mandates and accountability rules that we did not agree with, but I don't think that policymakers always set out to establish rules that are harmful to schools. I believe that sometimes good policy gets bastardized by school leaders. Hattie goes on to write,

> But they struggle to have the hard, somewhat uncomfortable discussions about the variability in the effectiveness of what happens at the classroom level and instead focus on policies which are politically attractive but which have been shown to have little effect on improving student learning—structural "fixes" such as more money, different forms of schooling, different types of buildings, performance pay for teachers, setting standards, privileging a few subjects, more assessments, more technology, lower class size, greater school choice, or longer school days, to list just a few. (p. 9)

Hattie weeds through some of the interventions and "fixes" that schools have done which have had little effect at all, and they are an important cautionary tale to new leaders who may be reading this book. The first example of a "fix" is by appeasing the parents. Hattie cites two examples, and the first one entails school choice. Hattie (2015a) writes,

> In the spirit of appeasing parents, systems promote the language of choice, although it is usually only the more affluent who can exercise any choice offered. The choice is nearly always a choice of schools (not teachers), and the typical choice is between government-funded and private schools. (p. 10)

Hattie goes on,

> This choice between schools is despite between school variability being, in most Western countries, small relative to the much more important, "Within school variability." This raises the question, Why do we provide choice at the school level when this matters far less than the choice of teacher within a school? (p. 10)

What Hattie is saying is that we have to be more concerned about the variability between teachers within a school than the variability between schools, which will be further addressed in the following chapter. This within-school variability is one of the reasons why I believe that collaborative leaders have to have instructional leadership as one of their top priorities. Leaders who are focused on instruction and committed to leading collaboratively can work with their teams to implement strategies that will raise the level of all teachers so that student learning is maximized throughout the school.

Hattie (2015a) goes on to write,

> These are typically expensive proposals, which the evidence shows have minimal effect on improving student learning. These distract us from implementing policies that can make a significant difference,

defined here as interventions with an effect size of at least 0.4, the average expected effect size for one year of progress in school. This commitment to the commonly heard list of fixes is part of the politics of distraction. (p. 1)

The other distractions that leaders are constantly hearing about but do not have a high effect size are "fixing the infrastructure" with more standards. Hattie (2015a) writes, "One of the major distractions to truly making a difference is the quest for better infrastructure: if only we had more effective curricula, more rigorous standards, more tests and more alternative-shaped buildings . . . or so the argument goes." (p. 13)

He explains by writing,

At the centre of any curriculum are the expectations of what is to be learned at various milestones. Setting these expectations is the power of curriculum (provided the expectations are constructively aligned to the assessments and resources used in classrooms). Too often, however, curriculum expectations are stipulated in "years," as if all students in a year cohort are working at the same level. (2015a, p. 16)

Continuing with the politics of distraction (POD) comes "fixing the students." This somehow paints the picture that students are broken and flawed, instead of looking at them as great opportunities that sit before us. Although he goes into great detail, Hattie's (2015a) following paragraph provides quite a bit of information. He writes,

When students fail to thrive in the early school years, there is an increasing move to "label" these students. Indeed, there has been a major increase in the number of children who come to school each day pre-labelled. (p. 19)

That labeling that occurs will not only hurt the self-esteem of the students and put them at risk of being on the receiving end of the fixed mind-set, it will also set them up to be tracked throughout their school career as students who just *aren't good at school.*

"Fixing the schools" is also part of the POD, and this means schools are always considered broken, much like the students within them. Fixing the schools comes with suggestions such as creating new kinds of schools, giving more autonomy, investing more money, lengthening the school day, and providing transformational leadership, which we already understand does not have a high effect.

"Fixing the teachers," is another distraction and it is based on the idea that somehow teachers are not qualified to teach. Hattie looks at many facets of fixing the teachers but focuses most on teacher education programs. Hattie (2015a) writes,

> These findings about teacher education have many critical implications, first among them that teacher education should focus on teachers being excellent in the first few years of classroom teaching. Teacher education needs to be about preparing students for the immediate practice of teaching. The recent push towards clinical models of teaching is promising, provided that the true essence of such clinical teaching is to provide new teachers with the skills of how to "Diagnose," how to have multiple "Implementations" and how to "Evaluate" their effectiveness. (p. 29)

Collaborative leaders can use faculty meetings as the central discussion venue to help prepare the new teachers on staff and, at the same time, offer new information to veteran teachers who have been teaching for a long time. There is a great deal of variability among teachers, and not just in their level of expertise in the classroom, but the number of years that they have been teaching. Faculty meetings are a great place to level the playing field.

MEET, MODEL, & MOTIVATE

As we know from the "Politics of Distraction," we often have the same recycled conversations over and over again. One way to combat that is to poke the hornet's nest by flipping some of these distractions out to staff before faculty meetings. For the following example, let's use class size as an example.

> **Meet**—Meet faculty where they are when it comes to class size. Most staff believe smaller class sizes are beneficial. Find an article about the benefits of small class sizes and offer an article based in Hattie's research around class size.

> **Model**—What is the size of your staff? Do you have the ability to engage with everyone? As a school leader, you have students, parents, and teachers to engage. How can you do it in a way that will model that it's not the class size that matters as much as what you do with that class size?

> **Motivate**—Motivate staff to have a discussion around the question of whether instruction really changes when they have smaller class sizes. Does their communication change? What about their feedback to students? How about behavior issues? Make sure that as an instructional leader, you do not get caught up in distractions such as prep time, class size, or just focusing on behavior of students.

FLIPPING OUR FOCUS TO LEARNING

Clearly, our mind-sets also need to change around these issues that distract us from talking about learning. We grew up in a system that focused on learning material based on the grade we were in, so we still have that mind-set when we approach how we teach children. As collaborative leaders we need to look at ways in which we can work with teachers and students to deepen the learning for each and every student and focus on growth more than we focus on achievement. Perhaps we have to work with the same curriculum, but instead of directing it toward the students in the middle and possibly boring the higher achieving students and losing the struggling ones, we should look at ways to level the learning to meet all of their needs. Collaborative leadership is about having these conversations with staff.

It was once noted that one of the worst statements you can hear in education or business is, "We've always done it that way." As a leader, I read a lot, and I still do today. I always tried to find research and books that would help me think differently. I'm sure you are like that as well. I feel as though we have to break the mentality that we have always done it that way and provide staff with resources they have not seen before because those resources may just help break that cycle of thinking.

In order to help improve the learning environment of students, we have to address the issue of surface-level thinking versus deep-level thinking. There is a great deal of research from people like Jim Knight, Graham Nuthull, Janet Clinton, and John Hattie that shows that students spend too much time learning surface-level knowledge, and not enough time going deep.

One way teachers and leaders have tried to deal with the issue of surface and deep learning is through the use of taxonomy. In the United States, we talk a lot about Bloom's Taxonomy, which has led to important discussions, but very few educators have come across the SOLO (Structure of the Observed Learning Outcome) Taxonomy, which provides a different way of assessing learning by looking for complexity in learning outcomes rather than a simple right or wrong determination (Biggs & Collis, 1982). Researching alternative taxonomies such as SOLO is just one example of how leaders can find new resources to help teachers think differently about learning. The blog post below provides a deeper understanding of the SOLO taxonomy as compared to Bloom's.

What's Our Best Taxonomy? Bloom's or SOLO?

By Peter DeWitt

February 18, 2014

blogs.edweek.org

Assessment is one of education's new four-letter words, but it shouldn't be, because it's not assessment's fault that some adults misuse it. Assessment is supposed to guide learning. It creates a dynamic where teachers and students can work together to progress their own understanding of a subject or topic. Assessment should be about authentic growth.

Testing in the United States is very different from assessment. I know that sounds absurd but tests have more finality here. When it comes to testing, we have a love affair with multiple choice or true and false. We test whether they know the ***right answer*** ... or not. Lots of tests are made of hard questions and easy ones. How deeply they know the answer doesn't matter, just as long as they know it. State tests focus less on what students know, and more on what teachers supposedly taught.

When it comes to assessing student learning, most educators know about Bloom's Taxonomy. They use it in their practices and feel as though they have a good handle on how to use it in their instructional practices and assessment of student learning. In our educational conversations, we bring up Bloom's Taxonomy and debate whether students have knowledge of a topic and if they can apply it to their daily life.

Interestingly enough, Bloom himself has been quoted as saying that his handbook is "one of the most widely cited yet least read books in American education." We are guilty of doing that from time to time. It's human nature to tout a philosophy that we may only have surface-level knowledge of, which is kind of ironic when we're talking about Bloom's Taxonomy.

For a more in depth understanding of Bloom's, the Center for Teaching at Vanderbilt University website says, "Here are the authors' brief explanations of these main categories from the appendix of *Taxonomy of Educational Objectives* (*Handbook One*, pp. 201–207)":

- ***Knowledge*** *involves the recall of specifics and universals, the recall of methods and processes, or the recall of a pattern, structure, or setting.*

- *Comprehension* refers to a type of understanding or apprehension such that the individual knows what is being communicated and can make use of the material or idea being communicated without necessarily relating it to other material or seeing its fullest implications.
- *Application* refers to the "use of abstractions in particular and concrete situations."
- *Analysis* represents the "breakdown of a communication into its constituent elements or parts such that the relative hierarchy of ideas is made clear and/or the relations between ideas expressed are made explicit."
- *Synthesis* involves the "putting together of elements and parts so as to form a whole."
- *Evaluation* engenders "judgments about the value of material and methods for given purposes."

The criticism with Bloom's is that it seems to focus on regurgitating information, and that anything goes. A student can provide a surface-level answer to a difficult question, or a deep answer to a surface-level question. It may show a student has an answer, but does it allow for teachers and students to go deeper with their learning, or do they just move on?

According to Pam Hook, "There is no necessary progression in the manner of teaching or learning in the Bloom's taxonomy." If we want students to take control over their own learning, can they use Bloom's Taxonomy, or is there a better method to help them understand where to go next?

Going SOLO

A much less known taxonomy of assessing student learning is SOLO, which was created by John Biggs and Kevin Collis in 1982. According to Biggs (n.d.), "SOLO, which stands for the **S**tructure of the **O**bserved **L**earning **O**utcome, is a means of classifying learning outcomes in terms of their complexity, enabling us to assess students' work in terms of its quality not of how many bits of this and of that they got right."

(Continued)

(Continued)

According to Biggs and Collis (1982), there are five stages of "ascending structural complexity." Those five stages are

1. **Prestructural**—*incompetence (they miss the point)*

2. **Unistructural**—*one relevant aspect*

3. **Multistructural**—*several relevant and independent aspects*

4. **Relational**—*integrated into a structure*

5. **Extended Abstract**—*generalized to new domain*

For a better look, here is a diagram provided (with permission) by John Biggs

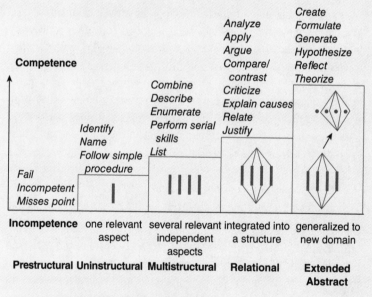

The SOLO Taxonomy with sample verbs indicating levels of understanding

Source: Created by John Biggs. Used with permission.

If we are going to spend so much time in the learning process, we need to do more than accept that students *get* something at *their level* and move on. Using SOLO taxonomy really presents teachers and students with the opportunity to go deeper into learning whatever topic or subject they are involved in, and assess learning as they travel through that learning experience.

Through reading blogs and research, one of the positive sides to SOLO is that it makes it easier for teachers to identify the levels and, therefore, help guide students through the learning process. Hattie suggests that teachers can use

- **No Idea**—equivalent to the prestructural level
- **One Idea**—equivalent to the unistructural level
- **Many Ideas**—equivalent to the multistructural level
- **Relate**—equivalent to the relational level
- **Extend**—equivalent to the extended abstract

Lastly, Hook (n.d.) goes on to say that there are some real advantages to SOLO Taxonomy.

- These advantages concern not only item construction and scoring, but incorporate features of the process of evaluation that pay attention to how students learn, and how teachers devise instructional procedures to help students use progressively more complex cognitive processes.
- Both teachers and students often progress from more surface to deeper constructs and this is mirrored in the four levels of the SOLO taxonomy.
- The levels can be interpreted relative to the proficiency of the students.
- Similarly, teachers could be encouraged to use the "plus one" principle when choosing appropriate learning material for students. That is, the teacher can aim to move the student one level higher in the taxonomy by appropriate choice of learning material and instructional sequencing.

Collaborative leadership is about offering new and research-based resources that will help change our old mind-sets. It's not that we have to "throw the baby out with the bath water," but we do have to look at our practices through different frameworks to make sure they are still effective. I used to send out e-mails with references to literacy blogs and classroom management styles, and then we could discuss them at faculty meetings. If I was to do it all over again, I would make sure we had deeper and more honest conversations about those topics.

STUDENT-CENTERED LEADERSHIP

Collaborative leadership is about getting away from the politics of distraction, and putting students and their learning at the center of our discussions. In *Student-Centered Leadership* (2011), Viviane Robinson focuses on five broad dimensions which impact learning the most from the leadership perspective. Robinson's work, much like Hattie's, is about putting students at the center. She lists the effect sizes of these five dimensions as follows: Establishing Goals and Expectations (.42), Resourcing Strategically (.31), Ensuring Quality Teaching (.42), Leading Teacher Learning and Development (.84), and Ensuring an Orderly and Safe Environment (.27) (p. 9). As you can see, leading teacher learning and development has the highest effect size, which is something that will be focused on in this book. However, the five dimensions are not always easily addressed because they are often very difficult to achieve consistently. Leaders have many distractions that take their focus off these five dimensions.

By collaborating with a learning team at your school, you will have more success at consistently addressing these five dimensions to positively impact learning. Without harnessing the power of your school community, you not only risk *not* achieving your goals but also burning yourself out too early in your career.

In a 2014 report titled *Churn: The High Cost of Principal Turnover*, the School Leaders Network stated,

> To achieve the leadership effect described . . . requires tenacious efforts by the same leader, over multiple years . . . it takes tenacious instructional leaders, who

build trust with a new faculty, set the vision for improvement and engage whole staffs in change efforts that are held over-time. (p. 3)

By grounding what they do in research that shows an impact, leading with humility and openness, and putting a focus on learning that includes all stakeholders, leaders can help establish a school community that they will want to help lead and see grow. Establishing trust and using open dialogue will help move that along a bit faster.

Robinson's five dimensions highlight the fact that leading teacher learning and development is the place where instructional leaders need to spend their energy. This means they need to work collaboratively. Focusing on the collective power of their staff takes leadership a step beyond being just instructional.

In the following chapters, you will find a plethora of ways to meet Robinson's research and focus on teacher learning and growth. Growth is one of the most important aspects of our profession, whether we are looking at students, teachers, or leaders, and it is my hope that the suggestions that follow add to the growth of school leaders.

Again, as you read the outline for each chapter, you will notice that I did not use the top ten influences because those influences may not fall into the areas that the schools need to work on. I have chosen the influences that, in my experience of working with schools around the country, are the most impactful for building collaboration in schools.

MEET, MODEL, & MOTIVATE

Meet—Depending on the level that you lead, there are teachers who focus on the politics of distraction. As a collaborative leader, it is your job to listen to the concerns to get a better understanding of where they are coming from, and find ways to refocus the conversation on learning. Meet all teachers where they are and begin turning the dialogue about learning around in your stakeholder meetings like faculty meeting, PLCs, or building-level groups.

Model—If we want teachers to talk more about student learning, then we, as leaders, need to send out articles, blogs, and videos focusing on student learning through e-mail to staff. Ask three questions in the e-mail that are relevant to the link you sent and then see how many teachers respond through e-mail or in person.

Motivate—Motivate teachers to look at research around one area that seems to be the anchor for moving forward in your school. Do they talk about how their children are different, class size, or assessment? What is one area that may be controversial, that you can start with to motivate all staff to have discussions to combat the issue?

DISCUSSION QUESTIONS

- What evidence, both qualitative and quantitative, do you use to show impact on student learning? How are you sure it's the right evidence?
- How does your staff focus on adult issues? In what ways can you help focus the conversation on learning instead?
- What influences do you practice as a school leader?
- What surprises you about Viviane Robinson's five dimensions of instructional leadership? On what dimension do you spend most of your time?

3

Collective Teacher Efficacy (1.57)

There is extensive research that shows school climate having a profound impact on students' mental and physical health.

Thapa et al. 2012

To Be Effective, Teachers Need to Be Motivated

In *The Global Fourth Way: The Quest for Educational Excellence* (2012), Andy Hargreaves and Dennis Shirley focus on professional capital, which they define as

> the assets among teachers and in teaching that are developed, invested, accumulated, and circulated in order to produce a high yield or return in the quality of teaching and student learning. (p. 49)

Hargreaves and Shirley go on to write about human capital, which "consists of the individual knowledge, skills, capabilities, qualifications, and training that contribute to a person's talent." In order to tap into each teacher's human capital, they must be motivated, and not every teacher is motivated enough to share their human capital. This is sad because teachers have to be motivated in order to motivate students to learn. Where do they get their motivation? Are they intrinsically motivated to engage students or are they extrinsically motivated by performance pay and points on evaluations? As a former teacher and principal, I used to meet staff, students, and parents where they were and work with them so we could move to another level. It's hard work, and I feel that I could always have done a better job. Helping someone grow takes dialogue and not one-sided monologue where we really aren't listening to one another.

As an instructional coaching trainer, I am often asked how to work with resistant teachers. The premise is usually that the teacher is resistant to working with an instructional coach and it's typically seen as the fault of the teacher. We are all 100 percent responsible for our 50 percent, and sometimes teachers are resistant to working with instructional coaches, or even leaders, because the coach or leaders put the teacher off in some way. Their personalities collide.

Most teachers and students don't wake up in the morning wanting to be difficult. Some do, but most do not. I think there is something driving their resistance, and it's up to us as leaders to figure out what that is and help them get through it. After all, we chose to lead because we want to get the best out of everyone that we work with. If we want teachers to engage students, then we need to figure out the best ways to model what that looks like by engaging teachers. Meeting teachers where they are is not always easy, but it is worth trying.

Some teachers, parents, and students are motivated from the day they enter school or parenthood, and others find a deeper sense of motivation while on the journey. Others have lost their motivation along the road for one reason or another.

Perhaps it is a parent going through a crisis, a teacher who has been in his or her grade level too long, or a student who was not treated well by a previous teacher or peer group.

We find these varying degrees of motivation in schools every day. We have teachers standing in front or beside students. We have teachers who are, or are not, communicating with parents. What messages do they send their students? What kind of conversations are they having with parents? Some parents will talk with the principal about negative or positive conversations they had with the teacher. But how many parents and students don't feel comfortable going to the next level on the chain of command? To ensure that teachers and students feel comfortable approaching school leaders, school leaders need to consistently work to build a school climate that is motivational and one that encourages open communication and collaboration between all stakeholders. The following vignette, although made up, is based on actual events that took place in a school. It is meant to highlight the need for collaborative leaders to approach situations in sensitive ways in order to maximize the contributions of staff.

//

Vignette: A Teacher Who Found His Voice

Frank Naylor taught 7th- and 8th-grade math in a school district made up of approximately 3,500 students. The math department in his school consisted of three teachers, and Frank very much valued the opinion of the other two teachers. One year, the team of three decided that part of their Annual Professional Performance Review (APPR) would be to engage in peer observation. Two of the three teachers were really invested and were looking forward to the dialogue, but Naylor was nervous about the situation, although he was on board with trying it.

Frank was quiet and often did not want to provide feedback to his peers. The other two teachers had no issue providing feedback to one another but they felt that Frank was too worried about being nice. As the principal, Clarice Owara had formal one-on-one conversations through the mid-year to discuss how the peer observation process was progressing; she found that Frank was not providing feedback to his peers. He always ended the observation by saying "Good job" and "I really liked it."

When Clarice and Frank sat down for their formal conversation, instead of just diving into the fact that Frank wasn't providing effective feedback to his peers, Clarice decided to ask how the process was going. When Naylor responded that it was going well, Clarice followed up by saying, "You are one of the nicest teachers on staff. I imagine giving feedback may be hard for you because you're concerned about hurting someone's feelings." Frank agreed and ended up confessing that he was having a really hard time because "Who was he to tell teachers what they needed to do differently?"

Frank and Clarice decided to meet weekly for a few weeks to discuss how he could provide feedback to his peers without "hurting their feelings." Clarice provided some articles on feedback from various journals that she found helpful, and Naylor started to engage in providing better feedback to his peers. Eventually, the peer observation process became more successful because each member stepped up to the plate and offered effective feedback to one another.

To encourage Frank even further, Clarice eventually persuaded him to join some stakeholder groups in the school such as Principal's Advisory Council (PAC) so that he could offer input that would contribute to the greater good of the school community. Through his involvement with PAC, he was able to help set goals for faculty meetings, and he ended up taking his new found voice and bringing it to his professional learning committee.

As an administrator, you will come across issues that prevent teachers from offering their voice. From this vignette, you can see that a principal approached the situation in a way that focused on the teacher's strengths but, in a safe and nonthreatening way, encouraged him to reach beyond his comfort zone.

By working together, they were able to solve the issue in a way that respected Frank's need to be kind as well as the teachers' need for feedback.

//

SCHOOL CLIMATE: THE PLATE EVERYTHING LIES ON

Parents and students will be more likely to approach a principal, for both good and bad reasons, if the school climate is inclusive and supportive. Everything school leaders do has an effect on the climate of the school. In an inclusive and supportive school climate, teachers feel that they can take risks with students because they know that, regardless of success or failure, their school leaders will support them. Within that support, teachers and students find numerous learning opportunities. Staff share their success with each other as well as learn from one another. It sounds like Utopia but it does happen in schools around the country.

The National School Climate Center (NSCC, 2014), under the direction of Jonathan Cohen, defines school climate as

> the quality and character of school life. School climate is based on patterns of students,'parents,'and school personnel's experience of school life and reflects norms, goals, values, interpersonal relationships, teaching and learning practices, and organizational structures.

According to NSCC, school climates need to be sustainable and need to nurture youth so that they develop into citizens who can be productive members of a democratic society. Rich and supportive school climates reflect values that make people feel safe socially, emotionally, and physically. Ideal school climates are collaborative wherein students, teachers, and families all work together to create a shared school vision. Educators need to model the joy and pleasure of learning to their students. All members of the school community need to be active contributors to the running of the school and to its outward appearance.

As a collaborative leader, it is one of your primary responsibilities to ensure that the climate in your school is just as rich and nurturing as the description offered by NSCC. What measuring sticks might you apply to gauge the school climate at your own school? What steps might you take to improve your school climate? Take one particular aspect, whether that be developing youth to be future citizens, school safety, collaboration, or love of learning—how might you take steps to improve your school climate on that front?

School Climate Suggestions

- Hang student artwork around the building.

  - Make sure it's well rounded and inspires conversation.
  - Encourage teachers to take students on gallery walks through the school to inspire learnable moments.
  - Talk about learnable moments and not just teachable ones.

- Make sure teachers are using literature in their classrooms that depicts marginalized populations (e.g., race, gender, sexuality).
- Encourage teachers to have student debates in their classrooms that focus on social justice issues (e.g., White privilege, #blacklivesmatter, gay marriage, etc.).
- Establish a Gay-Straight Alliance (GSA) where students feel accepted.

There is another more destructive side of the coin when it comes to school climate, one which creates an unhealthy dynamic between teachers and leaders. Unsupportive and hostile school climates exist where risk-taking takes a backseat to rule-following. Hostile school climates focus on compliance and not on taking risks in learning. This is more likely to happen in this era of high-stakes testing, increased accountability, and increasing mandates. Social-emotional learning takes a back seat to test scores and competition for grades.

Not everyone feels as though they contribute to the operations of the school. Sometimes that is due to the fact that they don't want to, while other times it's that they can't because their leader doesn't allow them to (DeWitt & Slade, 2014). Collaborative leadership, when it comes to fostering an inclusive and supportive school climate, is about the way leaders communicate with all stakeholders. As Todd Whitaker says, "When the principal sneezes the whole school catches a cold."

MEET, MODEL, & MOTIVATE

Meet: The main office has to be friendly and inviting. It's typically the first place visitors see (second is the bathroom, so make sure it's always clean!). When parents are met in the office by the secretary or secretary aide, you do not get a second chance to make a first impression. Even on the busiest days, the main office staff has to be warm and welcoming.

Model: Positive relationships and a focus on learning matter. It's important for collaborative leaders to model what it looks like to work through situations with even the most difficult of adults and students to get to the bottom of the issue, and at the same time, keep a constant focus on learning. Ask questions to get to the heart of the issue. "Seek first to understand then to be understood" (Covey, 1989, p. 247). After understanding the issue, bring it back to how it has an effect on learning.

Motivate: Encourage students to schedule meetings with you if they have an issue with a school rule. Even better, have them write about it and create a petition within their class. This will inspire student voice (see Quaglia & Corso, 2014a).

Enhance Communication to Promote Teacher Efficacy

Stephen Covey wrote about the emotional bank account in *7 Habits of Highly Effective People* (1989), and it's an important aspect to collaborative leadership. During the days with staff, students, and parents, and at night with partners, spouses, and families, adults have an emotional bank account. When we have positive conversations or really listen to what the other person is saying and try to help them figure out a problem, this contributes to the bank account in a positive way, which is considered a deposit. When parents stop leaders on the sidewalk to ask us for advice, when teachers come to us with a problem behind closed doors, or students enter the main office looking for guidance with an issue, we as leaders have the opportunity to make deposits. Every laugh or smile we share with someone is another deposit in the school climate bank account. Without those deposits, collaboration won't happen.

Other times, it doesn't go so well. Leaders may talk more than they listen, or argue to win instead of resolve, which is when withdrawals to the emotional bank account take place. There were times I made withdrawals when I was defensive with a parent and spoke without allowing them to speak, or I started a teacher observation meeting with the negative issues (nothing harmful or abusive). I observed in their instructional practices instead of the positive pieces they had implemented, and those all contributed negatively to the relationships I had with those individuals. Those situations slowly chip away at the school climate because individual situations affect the whole of the school community.

Collaborative leadership is about making more deposits than withdrawals, and as we know, schools are complex organizations. It's easier to make withdrawals. Leaders and teachers need to think less about winning an argument and more about finding opportunities for win-win.

Enhancing Communication Suggestions

- Notice something positive about students, parents, and teachers, and say something about it to them.
- Follow up with a teacher, parent, or student after a conversation that may have been rough.

- Follow up with a teacher, parent, or student after an inspiring conversation.
- Try to call or e-mail five parents a week to say something positive about their child.

All of these suggestions may sound "touchy-feely" but the reality is that they will help stakeholders feel more connected. Teachers who feel more connected are more likely to take healthy risks in the classroom.

RISK-TAKING AND RULE-FOLLOWING: FINDING THE BALANCE

As I sit down to write this, Twitter, Facebook and other social media venues are filled with something that negatively affects school climate, and that is the war brewing around high-stakes testing. High-stakes testing has enveloped many conversations about school, and is one of the biggest obstacles to school climate and how we conduct ourselves as collaborative leaders. It has divided us and created moments of withdrawals or deposits depending on the side of the issue we find ourselves on.

Large percentages of students opted out of taking the high-stakes test in the 2015 school year, and if the rhetoric around testing, evaluation, and teaching doesn't change, the numbers will increase in 2016. High-stakes testing and the movement against it have hit the mainstream, something I wasn't sure would ever happen.

Well before testing plagued America's schools, I believe our school climates fostered rule-following and not risk-taking. It's time to find a balance between both rule-following and risk-taking and put a strong focus on social-emotional, as well as academic, learning.

Based on an *Education Week* survey, Sarah Sparks (2015) writes,

Although survey results suggested that social and emotional learning has established a foothold in schools, respondents also identified challenges and needs. Just under half of respondents said their schools paid too little attention to social and emotional learning. More than two thirds indicated they had had some training in social and emotional learning and that they wanted more. In responding to an open-ended question about their greatest social and emotional learning challenges, roughly one in three respondents lamented that other things took priority, leaving limited time for social and emotional learning.

Collaborative leadership is about maintaining a focus between assessing learning, the demands of high-stakes testing, and meeting the social-emotional, as well as academic, needs of students. However, it also means meeting the social-emotional needs of teachers as well.

> Collaborative leadership is about maintaining a focus between assessing learning, the demands of high-stakes testing, and meeting the social-emotional, as well as academic, needs of students. However, it also means meeting the social-emotional needs of teachers as well.

In *Start With Why: How Great Leaders Inspire Everyone to Take Action*, Simon Sinek (2009) wrote about Herb Kelleher, the head of Southwest for twenty years, which was the most profitable airline ever. Even during the recession, Southwest continued to make a profit. Sinek wrote that Kelleher "was considered a heretic for posting the notion that it is a company's responsibility to look after the employees first. Happy employees ensure happy customers, he said. And happy customers ensure happy shareholders—in that order" (p. 83).

Taking Kelleher's philosophy, we should make sure teachers are happy in order to make sure that our students are happy. Happy students, who focus on learning, go home and tell parents about their school day in a positive way, and this makes less of an issue for school board members, who end up feeling happy to be on the school board.

We meet the needs of stakeholders by meeting them where they are, motivating them to improve, and modeling how to do it. By applying the Meet, Model, & Motivate strategy, leaders can do a lot to raise the level of teacher efficacy so that teachers who are struggling can steadily improve to the level of the highest performing teachers in the school. Creating a climate of openness and collaboration will do a lot to grow teachers' metaphorical bank accounts and also lessen the within-school variability to ensure that the learning of all students is maximized.

Within-School Variability

Recent research states the real issue when it comes to gaps in student learning is more within schools than between them.

In "What Works Best in Education: The Politics of Collaborative Expertise," John Hattie (2015b) writes,

> If we are to truly improve student learning, it is vital that we identify the most important barrier to such improvement. And that barrier is **the effect of within-school variability on learning** [emphasis added]. The variability between schools in most Western countries is far smaller than the variability within schools (Hattie 2015). For example, the 2009 PISA results for reading across all OECD countries shows that the variability between schools is 36 per cent, while the variance within schools is 64 per cent (OECD 2010). (p. 1)

Hattie goes on to write,

> There is every reason to assume that by attending to the problem of variability within a school and increasing the effectiveness of all teachers there will be a marked overall increase in achievement. So the aim is to bring

the effect of all teachers on student learning up to a very high standard. The "No Child Left Behind" policy should have been named "No Teacher Left Behind." (p. 2)

Hattie suggests,

> So, my claim is that the greatest influence on student progression in learning is having highly expert, inspired and passionate teachers and school leaders working together to maximise the effect of their teaching on all students in their care. There is a major role for school leaders: to harness the expertise in their schools and to lead successful transformations. There is also a role for the system: to provide the support, time and resources for this to happen. Putting all three of these (teachers, leaders, system) together gets at the heart of collaborative expertise. (p. 2)

This is where collaborative leadership enters into the picture. Let's review some of the ways to inspire teachers that have already been addressed in the book. This is not meant to be repetitive, but to illustrate their importance. They are

- Creating a positive school climate that puts a focus on learning
- Co-creating learner dispositions with teachers
- Co-constructing goals with staff for more productive teacher observations
- Co-constructing goals for faculty meetings to make them more like professional development, something I will dive down more deeply into in Chapter 5

Co-constructing goals helps teachers feel as though they have a voice (Quaglia Institute of Student Aspirations, 2015) in the school community which will help ensure a positive school climate. Having voice doesn't mean that teachers get what they want, but it does mean they have a place at the table.

FOSTERING TEACHER VOICE
TO INCREASE COLLABORATION

Teacher voice? What does that mean? Typically when leaders hear this term there is a concern that there is a small minority of teachers who seem to dominate meetings with their "voice." As collaborative leaders, we have to look at voice through a different lens. The extent to which principals encourage teacher voice in schools is directly related to how likely it is that a teacher will be open to collaboration in attaining common learning goals. Let's start first with a definition of *voice*. According to Russ Quaglia, teacher voice refers not only to the opportunities teachers have, to not only co-construct learning in the school community, but also to whether they feel comfortable sharing their opinions with their school leaders, and whether their school leaders listened.

> According to Russ Quaglia, teacher voice refers to the opportunities teachers have, to not only co-construct learning in the school community, but whether they feel comfortable sharing their opinions with their school leaders, and whether their school leaders listened.

That co-construction will lead to higher motivation. A 2015 survey (no longer online) posted on the *Finding Common Ground* blog asked teachers to respond to the prompt, "I feel like my school leader respects my voice." The results revealed the following data:

Q3 I feel like my school leader respects my voice

Answered: 475   Skipped: 8

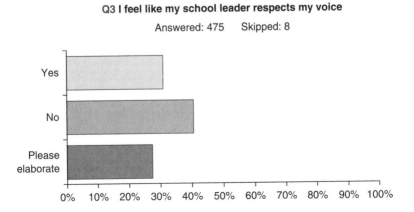

Around 31 percent of teachers said yes, while close to 41 percent said no. Nearly all of the 28 percent that answered "Please elaborate" wrote responses that "Sometimes" their leader seemed to respect their voice. It's sad that such a large percentage of teachers felt their voices were not valued within the place they spend so much time and provide so much effort. What can leaders do to encourage voice from those teachers who want to offer it? Leaders can do surveys to ascertain how teachers feel about the school climate, and then they can articulate the results at a faculty meeting, where they can also come up with an action plan. Not every problem that comes up on a survey can be solved but it would go a long way to at least address the results and discuss them, as well as try to at least change one issue based on those results.

The other side of the coin are the teachers who don't want to contribute. One teacher with over nine years of teaching experience wrote the following:

Teachers want leaders. Principals don't "co-share" their paychecks, so why do teachers now have to be made to be in charge of things like faculty meetings? Most principals make no decisions anymore it's all supposed to be "shared." I teach students all day, I don't have time to do the principal's job.

It was an interesting and eye-opening answer. Although we could all spend time psychoanalyzing the response, one thing is very clear; this teacher seems to believe that we each play a role in the school system and those roles should not overlap. Why would a teacher feel that she should not collaborate with her school leader? Why is the classroom seen as the domain of the teacher, and management and discipline as the domains of the principal? Is this a question of self-efficacy and how individual teachers feel about their role in schools? It may have been one teacher's response but it may be a comment that represents the voice of at least one staff member in every building.

The roles of teachers and principals are changing. Whereas it used to be the case (and still is in many instances) that some principals saw their role as primarily one of management and accountability and teachers saw their roles as being confined to the walls of their own particular classroom, this model is no longer an effective way to maximize student learning. In order to ensure that all students in the school reach their full potential, it is imperative that teachers work not only with other teachers, but in collaboration with the principal as well.

Therefore, we need school leaders who will foster voice for all stakeholders in the school. The best way to do this is to co-construct goals with teachers and host collaborative conversations about the changing roles of teachers and leaders. These conversations will allow everyone to voice their thoughts, opinions, and needs. Ideally, the spirit of collaboration will encourage all stakeholders to get on board with taking mutual responsibility for the running of the school. However, this also may be the opportunity for some teachers to opt out if that is their preference.

It is important that the conversations happen in a spirit of mutual respect and collaboration. We should not shy away from disagreements. The culture should support people who can disagree and yet continue to work together effectively and respectfully toward a common goal. Through these individual conversations with resistant teachers, perhaps leaders can get to the heart of why resistant teachers are, well, resistant. Is it possible to get them on board through offering resources? Resistant teachers may be so because they're afraid of what they don't know. At some point, the resistant teachers will need to either be left behind or be gently forced to move forward. The bottom line, however, is that if a resistant teacher is not doing what's right by students, it needs to be addressed by school leaders. I do believe that this type of teacher is very much in the minority and most teachers will rise to the challenge, especially when their voice is respected.

Getting everyone on board is not an easy task. It means that leaders have to create opportunities for teachers to share their voices, which takes a great deal of relational trust, which starts at the top. It means that most conversations, personal or professional, are about depositing into the emotional bank account (Covey, 1989), and it also means that leaders have to set up numerous opportunities for staff to collaborate. Leaders need the best from the teachers they work with, and that best will only come out of offering opportunities to connect and learn from one another.

Encouraging teacher voice also means that leaders are putting themselves at risk to listen to input that they may not want to hear and then trying to do something about it. One thing is for sure, based on the comment above from the teacher who doesn't think her job is to do the job of the principal, leaders need to make sure that they are constantly articulating why collaboration is important, which means focusing on collective teacher efficacy. Collaboration among staff is about synergizing to make the best possible environment for student learning, and everyone should be able to contribute to that.

Collective Teacher Efficacy

In a doctoral dissertation titled *Meta-Analysis of the Relationship Between Collective Teacher Efficacy and Student Achievement*, Rachel Jean Eells (2011) cites Albert Bandura's 1997 definition of *self-efficacy* which "refers to beliefs in one's capabilities to organize and execute the courses of action required to produce given attainments." Eells goes on to write that learning and change can happen even in the absence of successful performance. Furthermore, "mastery of a task is the most powerful way to effect psychological change" thereby changing a person's sense of self-efficacy (Eells, 2011, p. 19). Citing Bandura, Eells states that a person's expectations of their own self-efficacy in large part will determine which goals people choose to pursue, how much effort they will spend, and how long they will continue trying under stressful conditions (Eells, 2011, p. 19; Bandura, 1977, p. 194).

Fostering teacher efficacy in schools is the job of school leaders. Success in this endeavor will lead to a more inclusive and supportive school climate, which will in turn lead to teachers who encourage more efficacy in their students. By failing to promote teacher efficacy, principals run the risk of perpetuating a self-fulfilling prophecy wherein teachers who don't believe they can improve the lives of students do not in fact succeed at doing so (see Ashton & Webb, 1986; Eells, 2011, p. 36)

By meeting teachers where they are, motivating them to improve, and modeling the learning practices that will get them there, leaders can have an impact on the efficacy teachers feel. Remember the philosophy of Kelleher, which is that "happy employees have happy customers." Eells goes on to write that Patricia Ashton, Rodman Webb, and Nancy Doda

> found that teachers differ in efficacy levels, and the differences show up in teacher behaviors and student performance; that efficacy beliefs are not permanent and they can be influenced from without, by a variety of forces; and that feelings of efficacy can be difficult to maintain (Ashton & Webb, 1986). Efficacy is "negotiated daily" (Ashton et al., 1984, p. 380) and can be either threatened or supported by contextual factors. Efficacy is related to achievement, positive classroom climate, organizational structures, and high academic expectations (Ashton et al., 1984). (Eells, pp. 37–38)

Expanding on the idea of self-efficacy, collective efficacy is equally as important. According to Bandura (1997), *collective efficacy* is defined as "a group's shared belief in its conjoint capabilities to organize and execute the courses of action required to produce given levels of attainment" (p. 477). According to Eells (2011), "Together, people can accomplish that which one person cannot. Social action depends on the belief that a group can effect change. Collective efficacy helps people realize their shared destiny, enabling agency at the group level" (p. 51).

Take self-efficacy and collective efficacy into the school climate, and we come to collective teacher efficacy (CTE). Dana Brinson and Lucy Steiner (2007) say CTE "refers to the perceptions of teachers that the efforts of the faculty as a whole will have a positive effect on students" (p. 3). In discussing the collective efforts of the staff, we can go a bit deeper by looking at Michael Fullan and Joanne Quinn (2015) who believe that the group collectively has to share in a *level of coherence*, which they define as a "shared depth of understanding about the nature of the work among organizational members." Fostering teacher voice and co-constructing goals is essential to attaining that shared depth of understanding.

According to the meta-analysis researched by Eells, and supported by Hattie, collective teacher efficacy can have an effect size of 1.57, which is well over the hinge point of .40 that Hattie found to offer at least a year's growth with a year's input. How can school leaders meet, model, and motivate to foster a climate that focuses on collective teacher efficacy?

Collaborative Leaders Foster CTE by Doing the Following:

- Provide professional development, both building and districtwide, that was co-constructed with staff.
- Create a building-level stakeholder group that maintains a laser-like focus on a co-constructed aspiration.
- Encourage and require staff to share best practices at faculty meetings.
- Communicate in person or on the phone, and don't send negative e-mails.

  - Hold on to questionable e-mails until the morning to see if you still think sending is a good idea.
  - Remember that sending angry e-mails chips away at the receiver's feelings of efficacy.

- Have staff visit other like schools to see the teaching and learning practices of colleagues.

School climate is where collaborative leaders set the expectation that teachers will not work in silos but rather in collaboration to better address the needs of students and motivate them to exceed their own expectations. It starts with the self-efficacy of teachers, moves into the sense of collective efficacy, and ends with collective teacher efficacy. Roger D. Goddard, Wayne K. Hoy and Anita Woolfolk Hoy (2000) wrote,

> To understand the influence of collective teacher efficacy in schools, it is necessary to understand that teachers' shared beliefs shape the normative environment of schools. These shared beliefs are an important aspect of the culture of a school. Collective teacher efficacy is a way of conceptualizing the normative environment of a school and its influence on both personal and organizational behavior. That is, teachers' beliefs about their faculty's capability to educate students constitute a norm that influences the actions and achievements of schools. (p. 502)

It shouldn't be a surprise to anyone that getting teachers to work together will have a powerful positive impact in student learning. It is the mission of school leaders to meet teachers where they are in terms of efficacy, motivate them to move to the next level, and model how to do it. Goddard et al. (2000) go on to write,

> Additionally, administrators should be attentive to both the competence and task dimensions of efficacy. It is not enough to hire and retain the brightest teachers—they must also believe they can successfully meet the challenges of the task at hand. When teachers believe they are members of a faculty that is both competent and able to overcome the detrimental effects of the environment, the students in their building have higher achievement scores than students in buildings with lower levels of collective teacher efficacy. (p. 503)

School climate, self-efficacy, and collective teacher efficacy are about student learning. The focus ultimately needs to remain on our students. Through a combined effort, leaders, faculty, and staff need to develop a common goal to help increase the growth of each and every student in the school community.

In order to effectively prepare for the workplace and university, students need to be able to articulate what they are learning, how they are doing it, and where they are going to next. In Visible Learning training, we refer to this as helping students become assessment capable. Teachers who have a low level of self-efficacy cannot accomplish this goal. However, through collective teacher efficacy, the school community can ensure that all students become assessment capable, which is something that will be explored in the next chapter.

The following vignette from award-winning Minnesota principal Mark French helps to illustrate a few ways that leaders can encourage teacher voice.

///

School Story—Teachers Need to Have a Voice, Too!

Mark French, Principal of Rice Lake Elementary

Maple Grove, MN

There are research reports, opinion pieces, websites and educational leaders who promote the idea of student voice. Generally, student voice describes how educators should be inspiring and empowering students to take charge of their education. As an elementary school principal, I look to see how teachers are promoting student voice in curriculum, classroom practices, and other components of a student's day.

Teachers need to have a voice, too. They want to be inspired, empowered, and take charge of their profession. As learning leader of Rice Lake Elementary, I have used a variety of practices and strategies to give teachers a voice and incorporate those voices into our practices, procedures, and policies.

The first strategy I've used is to identify, delegate, and involve teachers. At the end of our last school year, my district, Osseo Area Schools in Maple Grove, Minnesota, was undertaking some major change initiatives, including grade reconfiguration for all schools. Each school was expected to establish and engage stakeholders in a transition work group. I took this idea further by creating work groups for transition, schedule, equity, student support, and school climate. I identified teacher leaders for each work group, requested the remaining licensed staff members participate in one or more work groups, gave some parameters, and let them loose to gather information, brainstorm, come up with solutions, and make recommendations. By empowering teachers and stepping out of their way, their voices were valued, appreciated, and heard.

Another strategy I've used to give teachers voice is to host optional listening meetings before the start of the new school year. These informal sessions can happen over coffee, tea, or a soda but the purpose is to listen to teachers' feedback. I use prompts like, "What practices do you suggest we continue?" "What practices do you suggest we delete, change, or adapt?" and "Tell me what you are proud of about our school." The purpose is to listen, gather feedback, and think critically about your schools' practices. This is a great activity to conduct as a new leader in a building and it is also good practice to listen to teachers every few years even if you are a veteran at your school. Next year, I'll be starting my eleventh year in my building and I'll be conducting listening meetings with my staff members who take me up on the offer.

A simple technique I have used during staff meetings or professional development sessions to give teachers voice is to mix up table mates. We all fall into patterns and like to stay within our comfort zone, but I sometimes mix up seating assignments. Each year, I create two sets of name plates that I use to mix things up. One set of name plates lists positions like "5th Grade" and "Media Specialist" for staff members to find a spot. The other set lists each licensed staff member's last name and I use those when I want to group specific individuals together. Mixing staff members up gets different voices into the discussion and lets staff members listen to another colleague's perspective outside of their grade level or team.

The most recent strategy to promote teacher voices has been to engage technology. First, I have used apps and programs such as Poll Everywhere and Plickers to solicit feedback from teachers at meetings. I generally do this anonymously because sometimes it's more important for me to receive the feedback and not care who gave which answer. I know staff members sometimes appreciate sharing their voice and giving anonymous feedback in front of their peers. Technology has also helped give teachers voice through social media. Teachers in my school are using Twitter, Facebook, Skype, and Instagram to use their voice to share thoughts, ideas, resources, student work, and events beyond the walls of their classroom and our school.

As a principal, I think about ways my supervisors gain my perspective and principal voice and I work to use those strategies, and others, to give teachers voice in their profession and in the work of our school.

///

MEET, MODEL, & MOTIVATE

Meet: It's important that we understand as leaders that not everyone feels we hear their voice. This means that we have to find various ways to connect with our staff. If we know that efficacy is an issue in all schools, and it is, then we need to find ways to make sure that our staff feel heard.

- Individual conversations where we listen more than we talk is an important first step.
- Take surveys and actually put into action the suggestions that arise.

- Hold faculty meetings where leaders walk in with one idea and walk out with a better one.
- Work with your school stakeholder group to get a sense of your school's climate. Is it positive and inclusive? Or hostile?
- Discuss the school climate at a faculty meeting. Put it on the agenda, send the staff the definition of *school climate* from this book, and discuss it at the meeting.
- Find a survey to use as baseline assessment of your school climate. Go to the National School Climate Center's website, click "School Climate" and then find the link that says, "Measure School Climate."

Model: We model good learning by being good learners—keeping up on research, using data in faculty meetings to have discussions around the evidence we need to understand our impact, and being a part of grade level or department meetings. All stakeholders in a school watch our actions. They watch how we interact with students and parents, and they watch how we conduct meetings.

- How do you presently model highly effective teaching practices to others? Do you take the flipped learning approach and use it at the leadership level?
- How do you model risk-taking? Do you purposefully try something new and share the experiences with teachers and students?

Motivate: We know through the research of Rachel Eells that we have staff who feel as though they cannot make a difference in the lives of students. How sad is that? They teach in classrooms filled with students and feel as though they don't make a difference. We need to motivate them through flipped faculty meetings, take surveys where we ask for input and then use it, and keep the lines of communication open at the same time we hold them accountable for student learning.

- How do you talk about learning with stakeholders?
- Who are your best teachers? How do you know? What are some instructional practices they do that will motivate others to try something new?
- Does your school climate motivate and encourage teachers to visit each other's classrooms? Visiting is only the first step. What do they do with what they learned?

DISCUSSION QUESTIONS

- How do you foster an inclusive school climate?
- Do you use your faculty meetings and stakeholder groups to engage in real dialogue around tough issues?
- How do you foster teacher voice so teachers feel like they have a place at the table?
- What is one action you can take tomorrow that will help build collective efficacy?

4

Assessment-Capable Learners (1.44)

In schools, great principals know that their job is not primarily to improve test results; it is to build community among students, teachers, parents and staff, who need to share a common set of purposes.

Sir Ken Robinson

ASSESSMENT-CAPABLE LEARNERS

It should be no surprise that just as collective teacher efficacy can have a large effect size (1.57), students setting high expectations for themselves also have a large effect size (1.44). There is a correlation here—teachers who believe in themselves achieve success and likewise, students who believe in themselves achieve success. Your job as a leader is to foster stronger and stronger senses of self-efficacy not only in your teachers but also in your students.

This chapter focuses on developing assessment-capable learning in students, also referred to as self-regulated learning. Assessment-capable learners are students who can assess their own learning. They take risks and know what to do when they don't know what to do. Using the language of Visible Learning (cognition), they know where they are going in their present learning, how they are going (getting there), and where to go next as they evolve as a learner. Assessment-capability is based on growth and not just achievement, meaning that each student's assessment capability may look different because it is based on his or her own individual needs. This research, especially the idea of student expectations, has an enormous impact on the role of collaborative leaders.

> Assessment-capable learners are students who can assess their own learning. They take risks and know what to do when they don't know what to do. They know WHERE they are going in their present learning, HOW they are going (getting there), and WHERE TO GO NEXT as they evolve as a learner.

When we think of our own students, we can identify a select few who are self-regulators, or assessment capable. However, chances are there are far more who are waiting in their seats to be told what to do. As leaders, we have to make sure that our school climate encourages teachers to not simply follow rules but to take risks by implementing new strategies that might increase the assessment capability of all students. A climate open to risk-taking means that leaders should make it clear that teachers have the freedom to try new strategies without having to worry that everything they do in the classroom will go into their evaluation. Teachers need room to fail as well as to succeed; otherwise, they will not take these necessary risks. The added benefit of this supportive climate is that teachers may be more likely to encourage students to take healthy academic risks.

The assessment-capable learning philosophy can be used for every type of student within the school. Every student, from struggling to overachieving, can learn to be responsible for his or her own learning. Students make gains based on their own skills. This means that students have the biggest impact on their own learning and teachers are there to help. Collaborative leadership plays an enormous role in bringing it all together. As a school leader, it is your job to bridge the gap between students, teachers, and parents.

When educators see the word *assessment*, they either think of formative assessment and how beneficial it can be to students and teachers, or their minds wander to high-stakes testing. Any type of assessment is important because it allows teachers and leaders to see where students are in the learning process. Unfortunately, in many cases the students are left out of that equation because a teacher doesn't explain what their assessments mean or what the students can do to improve in the future.

As a school leader, I wanted assessment to always show us where the students were in the learning process, but there were so many different types of assessments we were required to use that assessment became a serious point of contention. Two researchers have changed my beliefs for the better when it comes to assessment. The first is John Hattie. Hattie found that assessment capability had the highest effect in improving student learning. As Hattie stated, assessment-capable learners know where they are going, how they are getting there, and where to go next. This means that teachers have to involve learners in the discussion, and those discussions can help build independence within students so they know what to do when an adult isn't around.

To understand assessment at a deeper level, collaborative leaders should know the work of Shirley Clarke, a U.K.-based expert in the area of formative assessment. Clarke wrote a guest blog for *Finding Common Ground* in 2015, which helps better illustrate what formative assessment is and how educators should use it.

Formative Assessment:
The Right Question at the Right Time

by Shirley Clarke

May 8, 2015

blogs.edweek.org

My passion is the practical application of the principles of formative assessment—working with action research teams across the UK and the US to experiment with ways in which we can maximize student achievement. Formative assessment, through its unfortunate mislabeling, has sometimes been misunderstood to be continuous summative action or something a teacher does to students to get information.

Formative assessment is, in fact, a number of elements which **enable rather than** measure progress, and result in students becoming assessment literate. These are

- A learning culture of a growth mind-set (Carol Dweck) and meta cognition or learning "powers" (Guy Claxton)
- Involving students in planning units of work
- Effective talk and discussion
- Effective questioning
- Knowing lesson learning targets (confusingly called lesson learning objectives in the UK) and co-constructing success criteria
- Knowing what excellence looks like
- Effective ongoing self/peer and teacher feedback

Let's take one of these—the use of fantastic questions at beginnings of lessons, engaging students instantly in the subject matter and establishing prior knowledge.

Many teachers start lessons with recall questions and a culture of "hands up," during which many students opt out.

Once talk partners are established (my research shows that randomly paired talk partners which change weekly are most effective), the "hands up" can go, because every question to the class is followed by a very brief discussion with the talk partner. Named popsicle sticks out of a can are used to determine which pair then answer, thus providing maximum focus. Unlike the "hands up" scenario, every student has to talk and think.

Recall questions are often our default, so one aspect of my work has been finding brilliant question templates which can be used for any subject or age group. These can effectively convert recall questions into highly worthwhile questions which will deepen and further student understanding rather than simply measuring it, providing the perfect lesson start.

So far, I have gathered at least 10 templates, the most popular of which are:

- A range of answers
- A statement
- Right and wrong
- What went wrong?
- Starting from the end
- Odd one out
- Opposing standpoint
- Order these
- Always, sometimes, never true?
- Real life question

Remember that all of these strategies have most impact when talk partners are asked to discuss their thinking first, rather than as whole class. Let's take a look at some of them.

A range of "answers"

Notice the juxtaposition of "answers" which are right, wrong and "maybe." The more ambiguous planned "answers" promote the most fruitful discussion between talk partners. For young children pictures are used.

Which physical activities improve the efficiency of the heart? Discuss: *Cycling, walking, golf, swimming, skydiving, darts*

What makes a good friend? Discuss: *Kindness, always honest, shares their sweets, a bully, someone good looking, someone loyal*

What does a plant need to grow? Discuss: *Air, water, lemonade, chocolate, light, heat, sand, soil, milk*

(Continued)

(Continued)

The statement

The question here is whether the students agree or disagree with the statement, after short paired talk, giving their reasons. This technique can be used across all subjects. This table shows a traditional recall question converted into a richer statement for discussion:

Original, limited "recall" question	Question reframed by turning it into a statement for children to agree with, disagree with and say why
Which forms of exercise improve the efficiency of the heart?	*Exercise leads to a healthy lifestyle. Do you agree, disagree and why?*
Which metals are magnetic? Which are not?	*All metals are a magnetic. Do you agree, disagree and why?*
Why did Goldilocks go into the 3 bears' cottage?	*Goldilocks was a burglar. Do you agree, disagree and why?*
Which drugs are bad for you?	*All drugs are bad for you. Do you agree, disagree and why?*
Why do we need prisons?	*We need to have prisons. Do you agree, disagree and why?*
Why was Berlin bombed in World War 2?	*It was a good idea to bomb Berlin in the war. Agree or disagree?*
Find 45% of 365	*45% of 365 is greater than 54% of 285. Agree or disagree? Explain how you know.*

One teacher in a Scottish school showed her class a picture of a Viking and asked *"This picture shows a Viking. Do you agree or disagree?"* Those who agreed gave reasons such as *"His badge has a Viking sign on it"/"He is wearing a cape"* and *"He has a scruffy beard."* Those who disagreed said, *"He is not wearing a helmet. All Vikings wear helmets!"/"He doesn't have a sporran."/"He has the wrong sword."* At the beginning of a lesson on Vikings, students' prior knowledge and misconceptions were quickly revealed.

The statement can also become "Is it always, sometimes or never true?" such as in

- Multiples of 3 are odd numbers.
- Odd numbers multiplied by even numbers have odd answers.
- The heavier the car, the faster it will travel down the ramp.

Opposites, or one that works and one that doesn't

Being presented with right and wrong answers appears to give children more prompts, modeling and opportunity for thinking and discussion than simply being asked to work something out from scratch. Some examples:

Original, limited "recall" question	Reframed question, showing examples of opposites
What makes a healthy meal?	Why is this a healthy meal and this an unhealthy meal? (Given pictures or real examples)
What do plants need to grow?	Why is this plant healthy and this plant dying?
What do we need to make a circuit work?	Why does this circuit work and this one not?
What makes a ball bounce?	Why does this ball bounce and this one doesn't?
How do you do this calculation?	Why is this calculation right and this one wrong?
Who can grammatically correct this sentence?	Why is this sentence grammatically correct and this one not?

The opposing standpoint

This is a very effective strategy for discussing PSHE issues. Notice that the original questions are actually good questions, but follow expected and conventional thinking. The reframed questions force children to think of issues from an unconventional standpoint. Some examples:

(Continued)

(Continued)

Original question	Reframed question, taking an alternative stance
Why is it wrong to steal?	What would a mother whose children were starving think about shoplifting?
What are the hazards of smoking?	Should smoking be a matter of choice?
Why is it good to recycle?	Why would a plastics manufacturer promote recycling?
How did Goldilocks feel when she saw the 3 bears' cottage?	How did the 3 bears feel upon discovering Goldilocks in their house?
Why was it cruel to employ Victorian children to clean chimneys?	How would Victorian industrialists justify their employment of children?

Instead of asking *"How did Cinderella feel about her stepmother?"* one teacher asked *"How could Cinderella have helped her stepmother become a better person?"*

One usually low-achieving student commented:

"Cinderella didn't really think much about herself. She needed to stand up for herself. She just took it. She should have told her she was upset with her. The stepmother probably needed someone to stand up to here to stop her from being silly. She could have given her more friendship tokens or told her she loved her. Then her stepmother wouldn't have been jealous and might have liked her."

"Odd one out" and "What went wrong?"

Both of these strategies link particularly well with mathematics. I watched a teacher start a lesson on equivalent fractions, asking which was the odd one out among 1/3, 25/50, 1/2 or 50/100. Their responses on whiteboards showed that 2 children didn't understand, who were immediately asked to chat to their talk partner to see why they got two different answers.

For a lesson on properties of 2D shapes, *"Which of these shapes is the odd one out? How many different answers can you find?"* produced a wealth of ideas and clear indication of which properties students already knew.

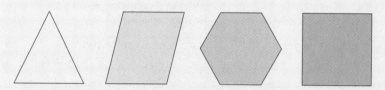

Using old pupil work to start a lesson with the question 'Where did they go wrong?' demands that students analyze and deconstruct, thus demonstrating their knowledge but also helping them reconstruct it. After learning about multiplication grids, one teacher asked the class what had gone wrong here:

| How much candy altogether? 26, 26, 26, 26, 26, 26, 26 |

x	20	7
6	120	42

$26 \times 7 = 162$

The mistake is not obvious, which means some thinking has to take place. . . .

The teacher from my second DVD presents his students with success criteria and an incorrect calculation for them to deconstruct.

So what did elementary students think about these questions?

"I like it when we have a question like this as it does make me think and you have to explain it. It is really challenging!"

"I think that answering 'right or wrong' questions is good, because it helps us to think more and we are able to argue against one another."

"I think questions are good because they give us something to think about and give us time to think and I also like that we hear what other people think."

"We get time to talk. The lazy people have to give an answer. It doesn't get boring for us."

Leaders need to be fluent in formative assessment. Instead of "faking it until we make it," we need to find resources that will help establish dialogue with staff at faculty meetings, PLCs, or grade-level and department meetings.

Leaders don't often include students in discussions about assessment but this can change. Collaborative leaders can provide the opportunities to make student learning the center of building-site discussions.

Before moving on, I want to address the elephant that is often in the room when it comes to leaders working in collaboration with teachers and students. A common criticism is that leaders are no longer in the classroom, they (may) lack a great deal of teaching experience, and/or they came from a different level (elementary in a secondary leadership role, secondary in an elementary leadership role, etc.) and do not have the expertise to tell teachers about areas of learning like formative assessment.

According to Hattie's (2012) research, teacher-subject knowledge is ranked 136 on the list of 150 influences, and has an effect size of .09, which is well under the hinge point of .40. This does not mean that subject-matter knowledge isn't important. It means that just because teachers have subject-matter knowledge, it doesn't mean they can get it across to all students.

Leaders are often in the position, more secondary than elementary, where they have to observe subjects that they may not have taught. Hattie's research on subject-matter knowledge shows us that leaders can still offer important insights into student engagement, and they can also find resources, such as those from Clarke and Hattie that will help the teacher improve.

STUDENT VOICE NEEDS TO COME FIRST

In order to work toward having every student become assessment capable, leaders and teachers need to have a deep understanding of their students. Where are they coming from? What makes them tick? Why are some so engaged while others are not? In order for students to be assessment capable where they can share what they are learning and why they are learning it, they need to have a voice in their classroom. This is one of the reasons why school climate and classroom climate are so vitally important. One of the comments that I often hear when I'm working with teachers and leaders on Visible Learning is that students need to take responsibility for their own learning. However, not all classroom and school climates encourage students to speak up, as much as they encourage them to comply with rules. Assessment-capable learning starts with voice.

> In order to work toward having every student become assessment capable, leaders and teachers need to have a deep understanding of their students. Where are they coming from? What makes them tick? Why are some so engaged while others are not? In order for students to be assessment capable where they can share what they are learning and why they are learning it, they need to have a voice in their classroom.

In their groundbreaking book, *Student Voice: The Instrument of Change* (2014a), Russ Quaglia and Michael Corso introduced educators to the Student Aspiration Framework. Aspirations, which can be seen as hopes, dreams, or goals are important for all stakeholders in the school community, but are grounded in the "doing," which means they are supposed to be goals that are actionable. Quaglia and Corso write, "Our aspirations affect with whom we associate, in what activities we choose to participate, and how we spend much of our time" (p. 13). Regardless of whether leaders work with elementary, middle, or high school students, they can agree that aspirations are important for students at any age.

An aspiration is that perfect balance between dreaming and doing. Unfortunately, too often our students don't have them because their voices have not been recognized or encouraged by their parents or teachers. Quaglia and Corso's QISA (Quaglia Institute for Student Aspirations) framework divides student voice into four different and distinct quadrants. Those quadrants are Hibernation, Perspiration, Imagination, and Aspiration.

Figure 4.1

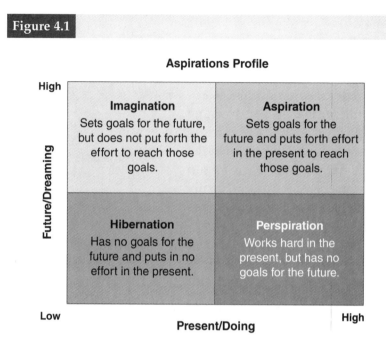

(Image courtesy of the Quaglia Institute for Student Aspirations)

Hibernation. The QISA framework shows that students who are in the hibernating stage are low doers and often try to float through the day with minimal effort and engagement with others. Like shadows floating along the sidewalk, these students are not engaging with their teachers and peers, and even more so, they are not making an impact on their own lives. Perhaps the school community doesn't care or try hard enough to find what make the students tick, or the students lack the aspirations needed to inspire their effort because of a home-life struggle. They enter school each morning and leave school each day making little positive impact on their own self-discovery. Students in the hibernation stage are not reaching their full social-emotional growth, which makes it harder for them to reach academic growth as well. Trying to figure out their social-emotional, as well as academic needs, is vital.

Perspiration. Students who are in the perspiration stage are doing quite the opposite. They work very hard and even get the results their teachers are hoping for but often don't know where they are going. They may show academic growth by traditional measures but if we measure growth toward our future or a purpose, there is a disconnect. Quaglia and Corso (2014) write,

> Perspiration is the category that describes someone who works exceptionally hard, always puts forth effort, but lacks direction and purpose. Those in perspiration rev, but don't roll. Such people are diligent, but directionless; they are busy, but see no meaningful future in front of them. (p. 16)

Imagination. "Those who can share their future plans but show little, if any, effort to reach those dreams comprise the category of Imagination" (Quaglia, 2014a, p. 17.). So many students, as well as adults, dream big but aren't able to follow through because they lack a plan. The implementation dip of trying something new often stands in their way. Any new learning provides obstacles, and students who fall into imagination stage are often plagued with a high level of dreaming but a low level of doing, which prevents them from moving forward. Like the movie *Groundhog Day*, students with high imaginations come up with something new to aspire to every day but don't follow through with the necessary work that is needed. Having a practical plan is vital for these students.

Aspiration. The goal for our students is to make it to the aspiration stage. Students who are in the aspiration stage are able to find a balance between working hard and getting the results they want, as well as challenge themselves enough to find constant learning lessons that help them grow holistically. In *Visible Learning for Teachers* (2012a), John Hattie refers to this ability as *Assessment-capable* students. They know where the sweet spot in learning is and how to remain there. Quaglia and Corso (2014a) write,

> With genuine aspiration comes the vision of a destination clearly seen and the passion for exerting oneself on behalf of the future. Such people have the ability to set goals for themselves while being inspired in the present to work toward those goals. (p. 19)

In order to meet the needs of the diverse students who enter our schools Quaglia and Corso believe that 8 Conditions are necessary. As you read them, begin thinking whether the Conditions are vital to the growth of teachers and principals as well. Begin thinking how they are vital to collaborative leadership. Those Conditions are

- **Belonging**—They need to belong to something but not lose their identity in the process. Being a part of a team is important, but maintaining your own identity while being a part of that team is equally as important.
- **Heroes**—Students need people to look up to. Everyone, even adults, needs positive relationships in their lives.
- **Sense of Accomplishment**—There is nothing quite like a job well done. Through engaging learning, students can foster perseverance and effort.
- **Fun & Excitement**—Learning is hard but we all need fun and excitement in our lives. For students, this can engage them in the learning process at a much higher level.
- **Curiosity & Creativity**—Engaging learning opportunities and a school climate that is inclusive and safe, which focuses on risk-taking more than rule-following, helps foster curiosity and creativity.
- **Spirit of Adventure**—According to the Teacher Voice Report (2015), "Spirit of Adventure is about being supported so that one can take healthy risks, trusting that it is all right to make mistakes and knowing there is something to be learned from any consequence positive or negative." In *Student Voice: The Instrument of Change*, Quaglia and Corso (2014a) explain that the ability and willingness to fail is a "critical component" to the spirit of adventure.
- **Leadership & Responsibility**—This condition is not just about the students who are chosen to be captains but about inviting all students to express their opinions, ideas, and concerns.

- **Confidence to Take Action**—When students have the necessary skills and support, and they are engaged through the other seven Conditions, they will have the confidence to take action.

Inspiring Assessment-Capable Learning

The Student Aspiration Framework is essential for fostering assessment-capable learning. First and foremost the framework helps us put our focus on students. Secondly, when we think of it through the lens of Meet, Model, & Motivate, we can look at each quadrant and formulate a plan on how to meet students where they are when they come into our classrooms and schools, figure out how to motivate those students who are hibernating or in need of a positive goal, and model how to do it. When we understand where students are as they enter our classrooms, we will have a better chance to foster assessment-capable learning.

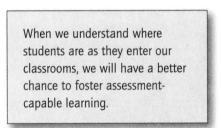

When we understand where students are as they enter our classrooms, we will have a better chance to foster assessment-capable learning.

This effort requires a strong collaborative leader who not only focuses on instructional practices, but who also understands how to develop relationships with students. Collaborative leaders do this by fostering voice in their schools. Some of the ways that leaders can foster voice include the following:

- Standing on the sidewalk and initiating conversations with students
- Having an open door policy where students can come to them
- Doing student surveys and explaining the results to students, which means explaining why they can use some of the student suggestions and why others may not be done (e.g., taco bar in school, recess 3 times a day, etc.)

Applying the framework to teachers may offer a better understanding of why some teachers have a low level of efficacy or hibernate when they get to school. If we can tap into which quadrant our teachers are floating through, we could use that insight to help guide our conversations with them.

Creating an aspiration for the school community takes the collective work of teachers, parents, and students in the process. It is not about *my* school but *our* school. This is easily done but takes a great deal of balance for this to be completed effectively. There are a few ways that this can be completed. One is that the larger district where the school is located may have a stakeholder group that represents the whole district community. Within that district stakeholder group, they may define their own aspiration. At this point, the collaborative leaders of each school can use their own building stakeholder group to define ways the school can take to meet the aspiration. A Principals Advisory Council (PAC), which I wrote about in Chapter 1, is a building-level stakeholder group that has a representative from each grade level, special area, and student group where appropriate. The conversation can be continued through PTA meetings, and school open houses, through questions such as

- How will this look for our smaller school community?
- What sort of resources do we need to meet the aspiration?
- What kind of communication needs to go?
- How do we plan out the year to keep the focus on the aspiration as well as deal with all of the other issues that come up during the year?

If school leaders are given the flexibility to create their own aspiration for their specific school, then the same stakeholder groups can be utilized. Positive school climates require that staff, students, and parents will be more engaged in and therefore contribute positively to the school community. When deciding on an aspiration for the school, representatives from each stakeholder group should be part of co-constructing the aspiration for the school.

Examples of Aspirations

- We understand what good learning looks like (Hattie).
- All students will know what good learning looks like (Hattie).
- We want our students and children to be assessment capable (Hattie).
- All students can define *learning*, and articulate where their strengths and areas that need growth are.

Remember, an aspiration is different from a mission because aspirations focus on the dreaming and the doing. Principals who are working toward an aspiration are one part instructional coach for teachers, one part professional development specialist, and one part relationship builder with students, staff, and parents.

The reason behind focusing on learning, and using the aspiration framework goes hand-in-hand with John Hattie's work. Hattie's number one influence on student achievement is self-reported grades (now called *student expectations*), which has a 1.44 effect size. Hattie says that his research shows that students do better when they have high expectations of themselves, which is why it is vitally important for school leaders to create a culture and climate where all teachers can work toward getting students to meet or exceed the expectations they have for themselves.

BE MORE THAN VISIBLE

I have written a few times in this book that leaders need to be more than visible. Being visible used to mean that staff, students, and parents could see the administrators walking around the building. If principals are not seen regularly, are they really doing their job? If principals aren't visible, are they effectively communicating with stakeholders?

Many assumptions come with the idea that principals need to be visible and they typically revolve around safety and discipline. For example, principals should be on the front sidewalks at bus arrival making sure students are getting to class quickly, in the hallways throughout the day making sure students are getting where they need to go, in the cafeteria in case a food fight or brawl breaks out, and on the sidewalk making sure students are getting on the bus and going home.

I firmly believe that being visible isn't enough. As a school principal, I worked hard on what I called my *morning rounds*—to be on the sidewalk for arrival and dismissal and in classrooms every morning to say good morning to teachers, staff, and students.

Challenge—As a school leader you want to be more than visible in the school community but you cannot figure out how to go just a little bit deeper, so you need to meet students and staff where they are.

Morning Rounds—When I was a teacher in a city school, Principal Mike Malet would go to each classroom every day to say good morning to the students and teachers. Years after working with Mr. Malet, that simple gesture never left me, so as a school principal I did the same thing. The students and staff began calling it my morning rounds. It sounds simple, but it isn't always easy to do because of emergencies that happen suddenly. But if you give it a try, you will find that it has an enormous impact.

Additionally, I was in the cafeteria or out at recess during the middle of the day, and in classrooms in the afternoon engaging with students and teachers. It was not always easy, and some days were better than others, but it was a commitment I needed to make. Why was this important? What does it have to do with assessment-capable learners? In order to help teachers with their students and help students move their own dial of learning, we as leaders need to build relationships with them. We need to see students learning in the classroom so we can be more engaged during child study team (CST) meetings where we talk about interventions. It helps us be more involved when we sit at parent–teacher conferences and can add to the dialogue around individual student learning. Being more than visible helps us build relationships one student at a time.

One example of relating to students was shared by Quaglia and Corso (2104b) in *Principal Leadership*. In the journal, they describe how both administrators and teachers participated in a program called "In Their Shoes" where the adults spent a day "shadowing a young person to develop a new perspective on what it is like to be a student. Teachers were expected to ride the bus, eat in the cafeteria, and complete homework assignments" (p. 31).

Quaglia and Corso go on to write,

Effective, student-centered principals know that students have something to teach them and must be part of any school solution. Those principals habitually seek feedback from students formally and informally. (p. 31)

These principals have student advisory councils, include students on committees and in department meetings, and poll students to gather ideas on how to improve the school.

Challenge—As a school leader, you are looking for ways to show your more humorous side to motivate students so they will want to approach you when they have issues. You're having a hard time connecting to students in various ways.

Friday Funnies—Our school always had a news program every morning. On Fridays, I was invited in to tell jokes. Students would drop off jokes to the main office and I would share them on air. Kids from all of the aspiration quadrants brought jokes they wanted me to tell and I would give them credit. The jokes were not always funny, but my goofy demeanor on air helped bring a laugh. I was amazed at how many students enjoyed the Friday Funnies.

Beware of collecting survey data from students without being explicit about sharing the results with them; it has been found that students become increasingly frustrated when they do not see any changes after they provide survey input. Students aren't ignorant to the fact that leaders and teachers poll them for their opinions and then often don't change anything about the school environment. They know when they're being ignored. Collaborative leadership is about making sure your stakeholders know that they have a voice, that they are being heard, and that their voice can have an impact on how the school is run.

Fostering student voice involves more than doing a survey. It involves interacting with students on a personal and academic level. Quaglia and Corso continue,

> One of the most creative ways we have seen a principal interact with students is by serving food in the cafeteria. . . . It can be a daily occasion to ask students questions and, after serving, sit with students to hear what they have to say. (p. 31)

Collaborative leaders need to create authentic relationships with students. What Quaglia and Corso write about is not unreachable. Serving food to different grade levels, welcoming students off the bus, having dialogues with them in the hallway instead of asking them "Where are you supposed to be?" or "What are you doing out of class?" in an authoritarian way is doable.

Principals have a real opportunity every single day to create the same kind of relationships with students that teachers do. One of the many powerful aspects of being a principal is that they can foster those relationships over a number of years as students move from grade to grade. It is through the sum total of all those moments that students will learn that they truly do have a voice and that the leaders in the school care about hearing that voice and nurturing it further. This requires a leader who questions the status quo and walks into school every day with the goal of being a change agent.

A COLLABORATIVE LEADERSHIP MINDFRAME

Hattie has written extensively about the 10 Mindframes he believes are essential for leaders and teachers. One of the mindframes is for educators and leaders to think of themselves as change agents. We need to approach students and learning from a more positive perspective. Hattie and Corso (2014a) write,

> Teachers/leaders believe that success and failure in student learning is about what they, as teachers and leaders, did or did not do. . . . We are change agents. (p. 183)

Hattie goes on,

> Teachers need to see themselves as change agents—not as facilitators, developers, or constructivists. Their role is to change students from what they are to what we want them to be, what we want them to know and understand—and this, of course, highlights the moral purpose of education. (p. 184)

Collaborative leaders can help support that mind-set within the school community. By providing resources and professional development sessions and fostering a school climate where teachers, staff, and students can engage in open dialogue around learning, principals can have an effective impact on student learning. Perhaps then, future research studies will show that the instructional leadership effect size has increased.

Mindframes for Learning

1. I am an evaluator.
2. I am a change agent.
3. I talk about learning and not about teaching.
4. I see assessment as feedback to me.
5. I engage in dialogue not monologue.
6. I enjoy the challenge.
7. I develop positive relationships.
8. I use the language of learning.
9. I see learning as hard work.
10. I collaborate.

Being a collaborative leader is not an easy transition for some principals because they either have never had a positive mentor or they lack the necessary skillset to do the job effectively. Besides their own psychological barriers, there are invisible barriers that still bar principals from entering into a teacher's classroom. Those barriers say, "The main office and halls are your domain, and the classroom is mine." It takes time, energy, and positive relationships to break those barriers down. However, it's vitally important we do because it is the only way that principals, teachers, students, and parents can make it through all of the accountability measures and craziness over high-stakes testing. Sadly, many leaders will not take those important steps because it is too hard and they want to take the path of least resistance. The post below was written by four school administrators in California who believe in being highly visible on their campuses, while staying connected through a plethora of digital tools throughout their day.

Leaders: Get Out of Your Office!

September 7, 2014

blogs.edweek.org

by

Adam Welcome—Montair Elementary School Principal, Danville, CA

Kenneth Durham—Sacramento New Tech High School Principal, Sacramento, CA

Jennifer Kloczko—Natomas Charter Elementary School Principal, Sacramento, CA

Eric Saibel—Hall Middle School, Assistant Principal, Larkspur, CA

Adam Welcome @awelcome

After first hearing about #NoOfficeDay on Twitter last year, it actually made me kind of laugh. My office manager always says "I never see

Adam during the day; he's always on campus, but we can see what he's doing by following our school Twitter feed!" (@montairschool)

> You can't feel the pulse or set the tone of your school in an office. . . . Embrace the digital tools that empower your smartphone to be the hub that turns the gears for your school site. . . . I challenge Principals to spend more time each day in classrooms than in your office, Tweet all the #eduawesome from your school, create a school hashtag (Adam Welcome)

There's no denying a principal has administrative "office" duties, I get it. There's just no other way to feel the pulse of your school without constantly being on campus and in classrooms. My first year as assistant principal and principal, I was in each classroom, every day, for the first one hundred days! You can't feel the pulse or set the tone of your school in an office.

What are principals doing in their offices all day? Your iPhone connects you with Google Drive, Remind, Twitter, Voxer, Evernote, and Google Hangouts. Embrace the digital tools that empower your smartphone to be the hub that turns the gears for your school site.

The "Adam" version of #NoOfficeDay is a Tweeting Challenge. This happens for me about five times per month and during my day I'll send at least three Tweets from each class. This is even more profound because our ENTIRE staff is on Twitter. Tagging my Tweets so teachers and parents can see what's going on adds so much to our school culture.

I challenge Principals to spend more time each day in classrooms than in your office, Tweet all the #eduawesome from your school, create a school hashtag (we created #teamkid) and increase the KDI factor on your site! (Kids Dig It)

Kenneth Durham @PrincipalDurham

As I head into my fourth year as an assistant principal and third year using the #NoOfficeDay model, I can say without question this practice transformed me as an educator and a person. My journey began after attending the Breakthrough Coach training presented by @MalachiPancoast. The workshop helped me articulate what I had always felt during my

(Continued)

(Continued)

eight years as a science teacher and struggled to convey to my administrative team my first year as an assistant principal.

How can leaders develop a relationship with students, teachers, and staff when we spend 95% of our time sequestered in an office? How can principals be instructional leaders when they rarely see instruction, or assistant principals become instructional leaders when they are not encouraged to immerse themselves into the learning process at their site?

California school districts spend approximately 85% of their entire budget on human resources. It is astonishing that more emphasis is not placed on developing the human capital of a district's largest investment.

In three years, I have visited over 1,100 classrooms and provided teachers with instantaneous feedback using Google Forms and the autoCrat script. When I began, I was told that teachers would resist the practice but found the opposite is true. If I walk out of a room and the teacher does not have their PDF in 15 minutes, I get an e-mail saying, "Hey man, where is my feedback?"

Even if you are not ready to do a complete #NoOfficeDay think about this: Spend twenty minutes in the morning in two classrooms and twenty in the afternoon. That allows you to see four classes a day. If you see four classes a day over a 180-day calendar that is that is 720 ten-minute visits in a year. Even if you only did it a third of the time, think of the impact that you can have on instruction, relationships, and culture in your building.

> If you see four classes a day over a 180-day calendar that is that is 720 ten-minute visits in a year. Even if you only did it a third of the time, think of the impact that you can have on instruction, relationships, and culture in your building (Kenneth Durham)

Jennifer Kloczko @jkloczko

Last spring, I was inspired by two "no office day" blog posts. To be honest, last year was an accidental no-office day because I wore many hats daily: lunchroom supervisor, receptionist, and even janitor. After reading *No Office Day* (Matthew Arend) and *Why We Love "No Office Day"* (Jessica Johnson and William King) I was determined to get into classrooms this year. Here are three ideas to consider for your #noofficeday!

Be a learner.

For me, #noofficeday is about learning alongside teachers and students. Each week, I'll keep these questions in mind:

- What did I learn?
- What did I notice?
- What do the teachers and students want me to learn?

Be present.

In "The Greatest Gift of No Office Day," Shira Leibowitz wrote,

No Office Days are special. I do no supervision or evaluation of teachers on these days. Instead, I participate actively in learning and teaching as a peer. Sometimes I teach a lesson ... Sometimes I provide student support ... Still other times, I am simply present, participating enthusiastically in whatever the activity.

Whether learning or teaching, be present. Listen. Write. Discuss. Celebrate. Connect. Dance! Last week's kindergarten hip-hop still has me smiling! My iPhone keeps me connected and allows me to respond if needed without ever leaving the classroom.

Be reflective and share.

Do I miss the classroom? In some ways it's like I never left! Instead of one class, I have a community filled with students, teachers, and families. Getting into classrooms helps me to reflect and learn about our school and to discover our strengths and areas for growth. Each week, I'll blog and tweet out treasures! Follow the hashtag **#noofficeday** and join the conversation!

> Whether learning or teaching, be present. Listen. Write. Discuss. Celebrate. Connect. Dance! ... Do I miss the classroom? In some ways it's like I never left! ... Getting into classrooms helps me to reflect and learn about our school and to discover our strengths and areas for growth. (Jennifer Kloczko)

(Continued)

(Continued)

Eric Saibel @ecsaibel

Be a Documentarian.

Leaving behind the confines of our offices frees us to witness, participate in, and record the learning taking place. Whether the medium is the school newsletter, e-mail blasts, or school social media feeds, the community has the chance to pull back the curtain and see the learning process in action. This not only gives our own community a more transparent view of what their kids' experience but also shines a spotlight on the incredible work being done by teachers every day. In short, being a documentarian means embedding ourselves in the process, noise, and hubbub of learning—and not reporting on it at arm's length from our offices.

Many teachers are also not yet fluent with social media or struggle to find the time to attend to the needs of their students while also documenting the process they are facilitating! Administrators have the opportunity to step back and capture this process to add to the learning archive of the school. By using tools like Twitter, Facebook, Instagram, or Audioboo for podcasts, they create a publicly accessible resource of what learning looks and sounds like throughout the year.

Get Students Involved.

We can also recruit students to document and share! We know for a fact that our high school kids are using social media—let's show with our actions that we trust them to use it as a learning tool by empowering them to be the eyes and ears of the school. One great example of this includes the work done at Leyden High Schools in Chicago under the leadership of Principal Jason Markey; he hands over the school Twitter account to a different student on a weekly basis, and students regularly contribute to their school blog.

> Recruit students to document and share! We know for a fact that our high school kids are using social media—let's show with our actions that we trust them to use it as a learning tool by empowering them to be the eyes and ears of the school. (Eric Saibel)

I found Adam Welcome and others through the use of social media, which has enhanced the collaboration I have been able to do, and has helped stretch my learning about what students are able to do. Collaborative leaders need to consistently find the gaps in learning and teaching in the school community; social media is a great way to help fill those gaps. If leaders are to help foster more assessment-capable learning within their schools, they need to look outside of the usual resources. Collaborative leadership is about strengthening the group, and it's not about doing it all alone. Social networking is a great venue to help get us there.

How do we focus on students who struggle, those who excel, and every child in between? We foster and support situations for stakeholders to collaborate with us and others. Michael Fullan coined the term *Learning Leader*. Fullan (2014) writes, "Learning leader [is] one who models learning, but also shapes the conditions for all to learn on a continuous basis" (p. 9). What I like about Fullan's definition is the word *model*. Collaborative leaders don't necessarily model the learning as much as they model what it means to collaborate. If leaders expect teachers to be lifelong learners, it's important that leaders show, in multiple ways, how they are lifelong learners along with their teachers and staff.

WE NEED EVIDENCE TO COLLABORATE EFFECTIVELY

How will we know that the number of assessment-capable learners is increasing? How will we know when our students are assessment capable? Evidence. Collaborative leaders foster a school climate where evidence is necessary to move forward in the pursuit to help every student become assessment capable. Sadly, schools collect a lot of data but often don't do anything with it.

Data doesn't always have to be about numbers. High-quality data can be either qualitative or quantitative. Hard data is quantifiable and usually comes in the form of some sort of assessment used by the school. Qualitative data is equally as important and includes information like classroom environment and instructional strategies. Cheryl James-Ward, Douglas Fisher, Nancy Frey, and Diane Lapp (2013) write,

> Collecting hard and soft data require that school teams and their leaders develop assessment literacy, meaning that they come to understand what the assessments do and do not measure as well as the validity and reliability of the collected information. (p. 3)

Collaborative leaders who are focused on fostering assessment-capable learning collect the data that will help them monitor progress, which means collecting both qualitative and quantitative data. They don't use the data to punish and recriminate but rather to focus conversations, collaboration, and learning.

James-Ward et al. (2013) agree with the notion that collaborative leaders who can focus on learning are vital to the process. They write,

> We contend that implementation and monitoring are all about building, maintaining, and extending the competence and confidence of everyone involved. And to do so, administrators need to see themselves as learners and to understand what it means to be a learner. (p. 4)

Challenge—You have a team of teachers who do not feel comfortable sharing data in the present climate of accountability.

Share Your Own—Collaborative leaders can share their data that focuses on their own effectiveness as a leader. Perhaps they use examples of the feedback they provided to students, teachers, or parents. Provide teachers with the foundation that everyone needs to grow and sharing data with others in a safe setting is a venue to foster that growth. When teachers do not want to share their numbers, there is a potential issue with school climate. Make teachers feel safe so they can take risks.

Adam Welcome, Principal
John Swett Elementary School

My top three takeaways for school leaders

1. There are many important characteristics for leaders to have, but without visibility so many cannot happen. In order to build relationships, you must be visible. In order to push change, you need to be visible and see what's happening on campus.

2. Empower teachers! Let them make decisions, collaborate with colleagues, give them responsibility, listen to their input. Principals tend to come and go from a school, teachers stay for the long haul. The more they feel empowered with decision-making, the more buy-in they'll have with those team decisions.

3. Don't ever forget why you go into education—for kids. Team Kid is a simple motto that encompasses everything we believe in at John Swett Elementary.

MEET, MODEL, & MOTIVATE

Meet

- Make assessment-capable learning a goal for your school. Understand that not all students are there, which is why you should meet them where they are, and learn how to bring them to a new level.
- Through the use of a student voice survey, the faculty can focus on assessment-capable learning by seeing if students are able to articulate what learning is all about. It also helps create a common dialogue among staff. Not every stakeholder has the same understanding of student voice or assessment-capable learning.

  - Have teachers look at the Student Voice Framework and discuss it. Even better, have them talk about a student in each quadrant and share ideas on how to bring the student out of imagination, perspiration, or hibernation, and into the area of aspiration.

- Have a faculty discussion around formative assessment. Formative assessment is not clearly understood by all teachers and staff.

  ○ Have teachers get into groups and have them share with each other, and then as a whole faculty, the concept of formative assessment. After the conversation is finished, provide teachers with a copy of the Shirley Clarke blog post from this chapter.

Model

- Model what collaboration means. Support stakeholders and foster collaboration. Share resources and send out articles for discussion.
- Keep encouraging the discussions on learning.
- What steps are you taking to realize your leadership aspiration?

  ○ Remember that the *doing* is important.
  ○ Does it focus on learning?
  ○ Who can you partner with to meet that aspiration?

- What does collaborative leadership mean to you?

  ○ Are you in a district that requires you to observe teachers two days a week? How do you model learning when you are in that situation?

- Join Twitter, Voxer, or Facebook (whatever you're comfortable with) to create a PLN and expand your thinking.

  ○ Join a chat session. For example, #satchat takes place on Saturday mornings at 7:30 a.m. Eastern Time and again at 10:30 a.m. Eastern Time for people on the West Coast.

Motivate

- Build community.

  ○ Greet students, teachers, and parents on the side-walk every morning.

- Do your morning rounds.
- Enter into the classrooms of teachers with whom you have a good relationship and watch the interactions between the teacher and students. Ask students what they are learning about.
- Have open conversations at faculty meetings about how they want to have more of an impact and help teachers by being a resource. Ask teachers

  ○ What resources do teachers need?
  ○ What are the obstacles of being in the classroom?
  ○ What do teachers want the principal to see when they enter?

Co-construct an aspiration for the school with staff and students. Focus on that aspiration. An aspiration is different from a mission. Aspirations involve the *doing* and include voices at all levels in the process.

DISCUSSION QUESTIONS

- What is the importance of looking at the effect size of influences on learning?
- Do your students know what good learning looks like?
- Ask students in your school to answer the following assessment-capable questions:

- ○ Where am I going?
- ○ How am I going?
- ○ Where to next?

- To get a better sense of the school climate where learning is concerned, choose the 10th student from each class list so you get a randomized sample of student opinions. Video them so you can show it at a faculty meeting and discuss.

5

Professional Development (.51)

School leaders and teachers need to create schools, staffrooms, and classroom environments in which error is welcomed as a learning opportunity.

John Hattie

WHAT DOES GOOD PROFESSIONAL DEVELOPMENT LOOK LIKE?

In order for professional development to be effective and long lasting, it should be co-constructed between staff and school leaders, it should have teacher voice as a key element, it should be ongoing, and it should focus on student learning. No one person can do as much as a group of people can do together. Leaders need teachers to help make the school community stronger. We shouldn't be working separately; we should be working together. This often happens with new district initiatives.

If districts take on new initiatives and then provide constant support through in-house professional development days and coaching to help teachers and leaders negotiate their way through the new initiative, then professional development can be very valuable. Helen Timperley, Aaron Wilson, Heather Barrar, and Irene Fung (2007) have researched the necessary elements of high-quality professional development which are

- It takes place over a long period of time (three to five years).
- It involves external experts.
- Teachers are deeply engaged.
- It challenges teachers' existing beliefs.
- Teachers talk to each other about teaching.
- School leadership supports teachers' opportunities to learn and provides opportunities within the school structure for this to happen.

The last element of high-quality professional development is often the most confused by school leaders. School leaders often feel that "supporting" teachers means that they should wait until teachers come to them and ask for assistance. I believe that in order to have successful professional development around a new initiative, school leaders should attend the same trainings that their teachers attend. After providing an instructional coaching workshop, I heard from the district asking me to come back and train their school leaders, which I had suggested should be done at the original training. They found that the school leaders didn't truly understand the idea of instructional coaching. The following blog excerpt provides a reason why it's important to have everyone at the same training.

[Excerpts From] Why Leaders Should Attend Teacher Trainings

by Peter DeWitt

January 17, 2016

blogs.edweek.org

When schools implement programs or frameworks, leaders and teachers don't often share the same room, which means that they don't get the same message and don't get the immediate opportunity to share concerns or become a think tank to create innovative ideas to make the program or framework... *work*.

For example, a district that goes through the process of instructional coaching sends coaches to get trained without the leaders present in the room. The coaches being trained have to go back to the leaders and explain what coaching is, rather than having the opportunity to go through the training with the leader in the room so they can form a partnership of understanding that will lead to healthier and more positive results as they move forward.

Professional development trainings that separate leaders from other staff doesn't allow for the necessary deep conversations to take place. It is difficult, if not impossible, to plan action steps to move forward because the teachers being trained separately begin thinking about how they have to ask the leader (who isn't present) for permission to move forward; this results in a lack of movement and inefficient back-and-forth dialogue that can prove fruitless.

Separating leaders and staff during trainings contributes to the dysfunctional relationship between these two groups. It reinforces a culture of hierarchy and mistrust which is toxic to a culture of collaboration. We have to think differently about the way that we go through trainings. We have to create trainings where leaders and teachers can work in partnership with each other.

Implementing big programs and frameworks takes planning. School districts shouldn't jump into them quickly. Leaders and staff together should be having conversations with the consultant or workshop facilitator to ask

(Continued)

(Continued)

why this program or framework is different. How can this help create better results than what we are already doing? What are the steps that need to be taken by the various stakeholders to ensure a successful implementation? Can we get all stakeholders on board with this plan? Having both leaders and staff in the room allows for a much richer and more productive conversation along these lines.

If there are bigger programs being implemented, then districts can create fairly based and authentically placed stakeholder groups where there are leaders and teachers. Fairly based and authentically placed means that diverse stakeholders are chosen and are not just the obligatory teachers who are going to agree with the leader's decision and cheerlead while they're doing it.

When coaches and building leaders work together, they are able to have rich conversations, clarify issues, ask great questions, and have authentic dialogue about how to move forward. That kind of synergy where everyone wants to move forward takes having leaders and coaches in the same room at the same time learning next to one another.

As I wrote at the beginning of this chapter, we shouldn't be working separately. In order to maximize the professional development that takes place around new initiatives, like instructional coaching or Visible Learning, we should be in the same room listening to the same conversations and taking part in the dialogue together.

Additionally, one big downfall when it comes to professional development is that it is sometimes seen as something teachers attend outside of their school building, or something that is district driven. We shouldn't always think that the best professional development opportunities are those that happen outside of school. The best professional development should be the opportunities and programs we create together within our schools.

I once asked a group of leaders whether they thought teachers should have a voice in professional development. One leader answered yes and said that he always sends teachers out to conferences when they need something. However, sending teachers out for one-day, off-site professional development isn't usually effective. Research shows that close to 90 percent of what is learned at traditional professional development like outside conferences does not work in the long run.

I was worried I wasn't being clear, so I asked it a different way. "Do you think teachers should have a voice in faculty meetings?" Another principal was quick to reply, "Why? It's my faculty meeting." That answer illustrates the thinking in many schools. The classroom is the teacher's domain and the faculty meeting is the principal's domain. This is flawed thinking because in order to have a school climate that focuses on learning we must look at all domains as belonging to all stakeholders and not just certain individuals.

Instead of looking at professional development as something teachers should go out to receive, we should look within our schools to the structures we have in place already— for example, faculty meetings. Using faculty meetings as a venue for professional development supports the work of Jim Knight, who has shown that with ongoing follow-up, like using instructional coaches, teachers can retain up to 90 percent of what they learned, instead of losing it. If your school doesn't have the ability to hire instructional coaches, an alternative option could be to use faculty meetings supported by learning through formal observations, walkthroughs, and PLCs.

Faculty meetings offer a great venue for leaders to collaborate with staff and learn from one another, but too often, they involve a sit-and-get interaction where teachers hear information that they easily could have read in an e-mail.

I once wrote a blog post called "3 Reasons Why Faculty Meetings Are a Waste of Time" (April 2015). It received tens of thousands of views and definitely made some school leaders upset, which was not my intention. At the end of the blog I inserted a survey (no longer online) and asked a few questions regarding the effectiveness of faculty meetings. A total of 488 teachers, most of whom had over nine years of teaching experience, provided some interesting answers.

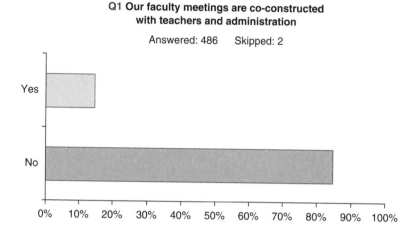

Q1 Our faculty meetings are co-constructed with teachers and administration

Answered: 486   Skipped: 2

Eighty-five percent of respondents answered that their faculty meetings were not co-constructed with their school leader. As a collaborative leader, you can change that by starting a Principals Advisory Council (PAC). A PAC is an easy way to encourage teacher voice, co-constructing meetings, and ensuring that leaders and teachers are working on the same aspiration.

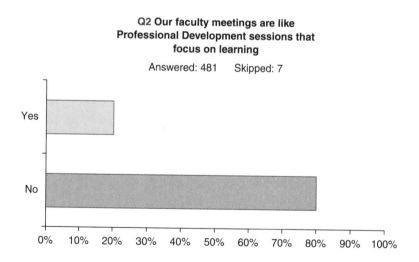

Q2 Our faculty meetings are like Professional Development sessions that focus on learning

Answered: 481   Skipped: 7

Likewise, 80 percent of respondents feel that their faculty meetings are not like professional development sessions.

If leaders ensure that faculty meetings are co-constructed around the common goal of learning, there would be healthier school climates. Think of all the progress that could be made if all staff took advantage of standing faculty meetings to learn together to accomplish a common goal—improving student learning. In addition to faculty meetings, teachers and leaders can also pursue professional development (either on their own or in teams) elsewhere such as via social media sites like Twitter and Facebook.

FLIPPED FACULTY MEETINGS

A few years ago, I made a concerted effort to focus on learning at our meetings as a departure from scrolling through the usual list of agenda items found at most faculty meetings. As the New York State Education Department (NYSED) began hammering schools with more mandates and accountability measures, I decided that it was my job to weed out the noise in an effort to focus on learning. To do so, I instituted flipped faculty meetings. I co-constructed meetings with staff through a PAC and then found resources to send out ahead of the faculty meeting so staff could get acquainted with the information, allowing us the ability to dive down deeper when we got together. The blog post below tells that story.

The Flipped Faculty Meeting

by Peter DeWitt

September 2, 2012

blogs.edweek.org

Principals set the tone every day and the flipped model could represent a symbolic way of telling adults that we still have to be innovative, and it's

(Continued)

(Continued)

really hard for principals to preach innovation if they aren't using it in the venues they lead.

Faculty meetings are as good or as bad as we want them to be. Some faculty meetings can be a time when there are great discussions about education and we feel as though we are a part of inspirational moments that we would only find in the Dead Poet's Society. Other times they are an example of bad behavior because adults have sidebars or they argue back and forth, or the principal is like Ben Stein in the famous scene in *Ferris Bueller's Day Off* where he just drones on and on.

Most faculty meetings have the same format. The principal sends out an agenda 24 hours before the meeting so the staff can see the list of items they will discuss. At the beginning of the year, they may sign up for specific months to bring food so the meeting feels more personal. I have some awesome cooks and bakers on staff so the food at our meetings is always top-notch.

Meetings where principals and staff get together don't happen as often as they should. Most faculty meetings last about 45 minutes to an hour and only happen once a month. A lot can happen in education over a month, so there are times when important issues can get lost when the new ones come up. Over the years, I have included quick videos to make people laugh during more stressful months. Other times, the meetings are quiet because people are overwhelmed so we get those over with quickly.

Unfortunately, I came to the conclusion this summer that my meetings, although nice, are not always worth the time the faculty takes to attend them, so I am flipping them this year. During a year with so many changes in education, I need our staff meetings to be different. They need to be more authentic and engaging.

Why Flip the Faculty Meeting?

"Innovative learning requires that you trust yourself, that you be self-directed rather than other-directed in both your life and work."

Warren Bennis

At first, it sounded like more of a fad than anything worthwhile. However, the more the cynic in me stayed out of the way, the more the creative side thought that this was a good model to use. Flipping the classroom can take the lecture out of the classroom and replace it with more in-depth student-centered conversations about important topics.

Teachers are using the flipped approach so, like any good principal, I sent my fifth-grade teachers the challenge of trying the model during this school year. Then the plan somehow backfired on me because I was sent a challenge through Twitter by a member of my PLN. He asked me when I was going to flip my faculty meetings.

In reading North Carolina teacher Bill Ferriter's (2012) *The Tempered Radical* blog, he posed a challenged to principals to flip their meetings and this year I'm taking the challenge ("What If You Flipped Your Faculty Meetings?"). A few weeks ago I researched different software to use so I could engage staff. I have done a few webinars and enjoy using links, videos, and PowerPoints so I decided to use Touchcast.

I was able to add pictures and links, and a 5-minute video explaining information I thought staff should know at our first faculty meeting (i.e., procedures, dates, notes from the office, etc.). In the recording, I told staff that we would be meeting on the first day of school in our first official faculty meeting to discuss APPR, Common Core State Standards (CCSS), and the New York State Growth Model more at length.

Those topics are very important to our existence as educators right now and the faculty meeting is the most important place to discuss those issues. Every principal and staff has topics they should discuss at length, so the flipped model is worth trying once to see if it makes those faculty conversations more authentic.

- **When doing the flipped faculty model, consider the following: Why are you flipping your meeting?** Don't do it because it is the new thing to do. Flip your meeting because you want to focus on a couple of topics more at length in the actual meeting.
- **How long do you record yourself?** It seems like 15 minutes might not be a long time but when you're the one talking it goes by fast. Unfortunately, when you're the one watching it may seem too long. Try to keep the flipped portion down to 10 minutes or less. Remember, the flipped portion is setting the stage for the actual meeting. It's not meant to make meetings longer but more productive.

(Continued)

(Continued)

- **What are you using to flip your meeting?** Principals have to use what they are comfortable with. I used Touchcast because it offered a free app on my iPad and it was very user friendly.
- **Who will benefit from the experience?** Both the principal and the staff should benefit from the experience.
- **What topics need more discussion?** During a year there are many topics worth discussing at length.

In the End

It's hard to step outside our comfort zones and try something new. It's easier to instead play it safe and keep faculty meetings short and to the point. Unfortunately we are teaching our staff that risk taking isn't worth it. That is the wrong message to send.

Our students deserve more than people who play it safe and our staffs deserve principals who will lead the way in trying something innovative. Principals set the tone every day and the flipped model could represent a symbolic way of telling adults that we still have to be innovative, and it's really hard for a principal to preach innovation if they aren't using it in the venues they lead. Try it once and see what happens.

This whole idea of flipping did not happen overnight, and I made mistakes. It took planning because not all staff members understood what flipping was, nor were they tech savvy enough to watch the videos or even understand why watching the videos was an important element of the flipped faculty meeting. Success also depends on being clear about your intentions from the beginning—let your staff know why you are flipping the meetings and why you are focusing on learning instead of agenda items. Flipping will not succeed if your staff thinks it's just a fad or a gimmick. Help them understand the merits of the flipped model. Send out an e-mail to staff explaining the flipped model and include links to articles and blogs that focus on the flipped model. Have a dialogue around the idea with your staff. Without teachers being engaged there is no reason to flip. Success depends on leaders and teachers co-constructing ideas together and working collaboratively to make sure that everyone learns something valuable at each meeting.

Other models include using Google Classroom to set up "classrooms" for different grade levels to provide resources specifically tailored to those classrooms. Another option is to use Google docs to make available all of the resources to be discussed in the upcoming meeting so that staff can be prepared for a deep discussion when the meeting starts.

I have seen flipped leadership evolve into something much more serious and important than the name may suggest. In 2015, I cowrote a blog post with John Hattie inspired by a back-and-forth e-mail conversation we had.

Flipped Leadership Is Collaborative Leadership

By Peter DeWitt and John Hattie

November 6, 2015

blogs.edweek.org

Peter writes . . .

Over the last few years I have thought about how powerful flipped leadership can be for a school community. It's one of those ideas that we have only scratched the surface of, and could have enormous benefits. If I was to go back to being a principal I would probably use flipping at a much deeper level. We need to move the dial of learning a little more in faculty meetings. There are many reasons why we, as leaders, should figure out innovative ways to engage staff in learning.

John writes . . .

One the one hand flipping is but the first part. Flipping is the tool for which leaders can engage in dialogue with staff, and staff can engage in dialogue with students. On the other hand it will never catch on alone. Just like project-based learning, which has a low effect size due to how

(Continued)

(Continued)

it is implemented, flipping won't work unless teachers and students have surface-level knowledge around the task. We all need surface-level knowledge before we can go deeper into the intended learning.

Flipping comes down to three key aspects.

1. First, leaders need to work in collaboration with students and teachers early to show what success in a task might look like, which is referred to as "success criteria." This will provide them with subject-matter vocabulary that they need, but it is a big shift in thinking for many educators and students. Very often students don't know what success looks like until after the teacher gives them a grade. And sometimes even then they are left wondering because no dialogue takes place after.

    Additionally, teachers don't know what their leader's version of success looks like until after their evaluation is completed by their principal. Even after the evaluation process, the teacher may be unclear because the feedback may not offer enough to move the learning forward. Or worse, the evaluation only offers praise.

2. Secondly, we need to allow students and teachers to understand what learning is all about. At the faculty level, what dialogue has happened with teachers around what good learning looks like?

    Does the leader know?

    Can the school leader and staff develop an understanding together?

    In writing the Politics of Distraction, which addresses the fact that we spend too much time talking about adult issues, I suggested that leaders and faculty have to spend time having dialogue around what good learning looks like. Too often children think a good learner is someone who sits in their seat, raises their hand, and waits for the teacher to give them the next direction. That's compliance . . . not learning.

3. Lastly, flipped leadership and flipped learning is supposed to encourage dialogue, deliberate teaching, the giving and receiving of feedback, and a focus on deliberate practice. That deliberate practice,

whether we are talking about teachers at a faculty meeting or students in the classroom, should be a mix of surface and deep learning and practicing transfer.

> Flipped leadership and flipped learning is supposed to encourage dialogue, deliberate teaching, the giving and receiving of feedback, and a focus on deliberate practice.

If principals are merely sending out a resource like a video or blog that only supports their way of thinking, then true dialogue may not take place. Furthermore, if leaders walk into faculty meetings with one idea and walk out with the same one, real authentic dialogue never took place. The following graphic illustrates the **"Cycle of Collaborative Leadership"** that flipping needs.

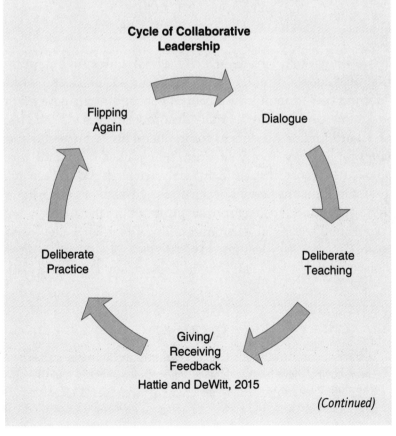

Cycle of Collaborative Leadership

Flipping Again

Dialogue

Deliberate Practice

Deliberate Teaching

Giving/ Receiving Feedback

Hattie and DeWitt, 2015

(Continued)

(Continued)

Flipping for the sake of flipping will burn out before it ever reaches its full potential.

In the End

In order for flipped leadership and flipped learning to work, teachers need to understand why it is necessary, what work needs to be done to truly get an understanding of whatever topic has been co-constructed with staff, and how to do it in a way that will deepen the learning.

Flipped leadership done correctly should be seen as collaborative leadership . . .

COLLABORATIVE LEADERS
DEBATE, DISSECT, AND DISCUSS

When I taught 2nd grade in a city school with a high population of students receiving free and reduced lunch, the word "decompose" came up as a central concept in our new math program. It seemed to me that "decompose" was way too big of a word for 2nd graders to comprehend but went ahead and taught it anyway. To my surprise, they picked it up and were able to use it correctly. Unfortunately, we leaders don't always give staff the same benefit of the doubt. Instead of giving them the opportunity to decompose information themselves, we spend time talking at them and telling them what they need to do. Collaborative leaders do not do that. They guide discussions by doing what I call Debate, Dissect, and Discuss (3 Ds!).

The 3 Ds!

Debate—In a positive, supportive, and inclusive school climate, staff are encouraged to have healthy debate. Confrontation is only a bad thing if it doesn't lead to something more positive. This doesn't mean that staff can break out into a brawl, and norms do have to be established.

If one faculty member feels as though the rest are against him or her it can lead to some hard feelings. Collaborative leaders find a balance for these debates so people can get their feelings out in the open. Anything else builds resentment and we never move forward when resentment is in the air.

Dissect—Many school leaders do a great job of allowing their staff to break down curriculum during grade level meetings, but this isn't just about curriculum. We need to dissect our approaches to student learning. For example, on the topic of Feedback, Hattie writes, "70% of teachers claimed that they provided detailed feedback that helped students improve their next assignments." The problem was that only "45% of students agreed with their teachers' claims (2009. p. 138)." Feedback is something schools think they do well but their application is not always as good as they believe. It would be great to take a faculty meeting or two and dedicate it to feedback. Staff need to bring in their examples of what feedback looks like in their classroom. As a group they can each dissect their own styles of feedback as well as their colleagues' styles to get a better sense of the pros and cons of various approaches.

Discussion—These robust discussions can help teachers get a better understanding of the feedback they provide to students. We need to engage in more discussions with our colleagues and PACs to come up with ways to improve the feedback teachers give to students and to collectively think of ways to make that feedback more transparent.

One of the ways that leaders can help foster this with teachers is through the use of collaborative inquiry. Collaborative inquiry is a high-quality professional learning design that incorporates teachers' voices and draws on the expertise and experiences of the faculty. Donohoo (2013) outlined a four-stage model in which teams identify student learning needs and develop a question about a particular link between professional practice and student results. Teachers test new approaches in their classrooms while gathering evidence and artifacts. Next, teams collectively analyze data to assess the impact of their actions and finally, they determine their next steps.

Ultimately, collaborative inquiry serves as an alternative to short-term, top-down, formulaic approaches to professional learning that do not hold enough rigor to realize self-sustaining cycles of improvement in schools (Donohoo & Velasco, 2016). Collaborative inquiry supports the notion of teacher leadership as it recognizes the role of teachers in on-going school improvement.

Collaborative leadership is not always about being the one who leads the discussion. It is about finding teacher leaders who can share their expertise. Collaborative leadership and collaborative inquiry both focus on deep learning. Times are tough and school leaders can't get into classes all of the time. But they can get a better understanding of the learning taking place in school by having robust faculty meetings, strong professional learning communities (PLCs), or collaborative inquiry, where staff can debate, dissect, and discuss student learning.

This is not easy because it means that leaders need to help those staff with a low level of self-efficacy in order to make sure that all teachers contribute to the ongoing conversations around learning. One of the other ways to look at this issue of self-efficacy and teacher contributions is through the lens of Russ Quaglia's work on student voice. I understand that seems like an odd comparison, but let me explain.

Just as students fall into the hibernation, imagination, perspiration, or aspiration stage, we know that principals, teachers, and even parents do also (see Chapter 4, Figure 4.1). We have students, parents, and teachers working hard with no goal in mind: We have students and teachers in the hibernation stage where they just want to come into school and disappear into their classrooms or parents in the hibernation stage who want to quickly drop their children off at school without engaging in conversation with school staff.

The worst is when principals want to stay in the hibernation stage and hide in their offices so they don't have to engage in difficult conversations. Those principals who fall into the hibernation stage are more likely to be the principals who fall into the bystander quadrant of the collaborative leadership profile because they will let others take over so they don't have to make hard decisions. This does nothing to bring out collective teacher efficacy.

Collaborative leaders can help bring all stakeholders to the Aspiration stage by ensuring that all of the 8 Conditions vital to a healthy school climate are present (see Chapter 4).

THE CORE BUSINESS OF LEARNING

Hattie's philosophy about the politics of distraction is the main reason why I believe that a focus on learning through professional development in the school environment is the first key to collaborative leadership. Everyone who works in a school should put learning at the center of what they do. Hattie often asks educators whether they have the word *learning* on the first page of their school website or in their school's mission and vision statement. The reality, and much of what POD (the politics of distraction) is about, is that it's not as easy for leaders and teachers to put learning at the center of their conversations. When a principal and teacher have discussions about schools, it mostly likely focuses on student behavior and discipline issues.

As you know from Chapter 2, the politics of distraction prevent us from talking about learning. Those distractions may include prep time, contractual time, Annual Professional Performance Review (APPR), the bell schedule, teacher observations, or high-stakes testing. They prevent us from discussing how to increase learning opportunities for students that foster collaboration and real dialogue among peers. Perhaps it is easier to talk about the politics of distraction because talking about learning is really difficult. Hattie (2012a) writes,

> Learning is not always pleasurable and easy; it requires over-learning at certain points, spiraling up and down the knowledge continuum, building a working relationship with others in grappling with challenging

tasks. Students appreciate that learning is not always pleasurable and easy, and indeed engage with and enjoy the challenges that learning entails. (p. 17)

The same can be said for adult learning in schools. It's not always pleasurable to walk into a meeting to talk about learning. We also understand that when people feel passionate about a subject, which teachers do, some of those adults react in conflicting ways. I have been a part of many curriculum meetings where teachers wanted to discuss learning and when it went into debate mode, some teachers retracted from the conversation because they didn't like the direction or tone of the conversation.

The job of the collaborative leader is to create a climate where the difficult discussions about learning can happen in deep, meaningful, and safe ways. Ask "What does good learning look like? How can all students achieve good learning, and define it on their own?" Equally as important to student understanding is that teachers can define, understand, and recognize good learning as well.

It may sound like common sense but it's actually a bit more complicated than you may think. I see teachers who define *good learning* by the behavior of the students. To them, good learning is about students sitting in their seats, raising their hands, and doing what the teachers say. On the other hand, there are many teachers who clearly understand what good learning looks like. They talk about it with students, look for it on a daily basis, and can hone in on those times when it's not happening. The difference between teachers who look at it through the behavioral lens and those who look at

> The job of the collaborative leader is to create a climate where the difficult discussions about learning can happen in deep, meaningful, and safe ways. Ask "What does good learning look like? How can all students achieve good learning, and define it on their own?" Equally as important to student understanding is that teachers can define, understand, and recognize good learning as well.

it through a pedagogical one can be quite significant; and I'm not referring to teachers who work in one school as opposed to another. I'm referring to teachers who work in the same school *with* one another. Keeping the focus on learning rather than discipline issues that may or may not exist is really a challenge for collaborative leaders.

It's important to remember that when fostering professional growth as a collaborative leader, principals need to reflect on three areas.

1. **As a principal, what quadrant of the student voice framework describes you best?**

2. **How is your aspiration tied to student learning?**

3. **How deep do the politics of distraction go in your school? Do you focus on adult issues in daily conversations more than student learning?**

As a collaborative leader, ask yourself, "What can I do to refocus the staff's attention on student learning?"

Challenge—As much as leaders want to focus on learning, they spend a great deal of time being reactive rather than proactive. Despite the best of intentions, faculty meetings fall back into the pattern of going through a list of tasks.

Solution—It doesn't matter where you are in the school year, stop having list-of-tasks meetings. Share a blog post on flipped faculty meetings and have a conversation with the staff. Ask "What would you want to learn about at the next meeting? What are the common themes that come up in the hallway, closed door meetings, or in the faculty room?" Really listen. Together come up with a topic to learn about and explore. Choose one to three great articles on the topic; ask staff to also look for relevant articles to share. Send the articles to staff ahead of the next meeting and ask them to be prepared for the discussion. Build on that learning for every meeting.

Learning is the core business of schools.

John Hattie

A focus on learning is the most important key for instructional leaders because it provides the basis for their focus every day, and that includes professional learning as well. It's not to say collaborative leaders can't have more personal conversations with staff, but learning should be at the heart of most of the conversations.

The meetings that most school leaders already have in place provide the opportunity to talk about learning. It doesn't happen overnight. Collaborative leaders need to foster a climate of risk-taking and not just rule-following so teachers feel as though they have more of a voice. They also need to be able to discuss with staff the reasons they are flipping their meetings in an effort to focus on professional learning. These strategies could lead to really powerful professional learning and thereafter real improvement in student learning schoolwide.

//

School Story—Using Research to Engage All Stakeholders

Catherine Worley, Principal of Jamestown High School

Williamsburg, VA

As a school leader, providing quality professional development for teachers is always a top priority. Educational mandates and practices are constantly changing; therefore, leaders need to constantly provide evolving and applicable professional development for teachers. We are living through the era of accountability and high-stakes testing, but at the end of the day, we have to ask ourselves the question "How is this impacting our kids?" It's our obligation to facilitate opportunities for all students to be successful, graduate, and become responsible citizens and leaders of our society. We need robust professional development to make sure that we are all providing those learning opportunities for students.

As the Jamestown High School principal in Williamsburg, Virginia, with over 25 years of experience in K–12 education, I face many new challenges each year.

As a leader who strives to study current research and implement best practices, I began reading about the work and research of John Hattie in 2010. We all know that students learn in different ways. Long gone should be the days of hour lectures or the infamous "sit and get" sessions. John Hattie's research confirms and supports the need for intervention in how learning takes place in the classroom. I have always told my teachers, "The one doing the work is the one doing the learning." We have to continue to facilitate student-led learning opportunities with options for choice and collaboration. We need professional development to help us get there. Professional learning networks (PLNs) can be a rich source of professional development.

Although my current high school is high performing within our district and state, we are facing challenges and need to implement strategies to close achievement gaps and ensure all of our students graduate. Our school division has a partnership with SURN (School University Research Network) at William and Mary. This network has allowed me the wonderful opportunity to collaborate with leaders around the state, as well as serve as a principal mentor for new administrators. Since my involvement with SURN in July of 2012, I have been provided with many resources to support moving my school forward. These include books for book studies, walk-through forms that directly correlate with High Yield Instructional Strategies (HYIS), and other resources that supplement the research of John Hattie to use within my school.

Good instruction that facilitates student engagement, critical thinking, curiosity, problem-solving, collaboration, and the ability/desire to become lifelong learners is paramount. Over the past three and one-half years at JHS, we have researched, discussed, and collaborated to implement best practices and HYIS that we know will make the biggest impact on student achievement. The table below outlines some of our ongoing professional development and PLN work.

Best Practices and High Yield Instructional Strategies Implemented at Jamestown High School

What	When	Summary
Book Studies	2013–2014 2014–2015 2015–2016	Teachers volunteer to participate in book studies and then present information in faculty meetings. We started with *Visible Learning for Teachers*, and moved to *Visible Learning and the Science of How We Learn*.
Walk-Throughs	2013–Current	We implemented two walk-through forms created through our partnership with SURN. The forms are correlated with John Hattie's research on instructional strategies. The forms allow the observer to check which high- or low-yield strategies were observed as well as to note examples of the strategies observed. The Student Engagement tool collects data on what the students are doing. The HYIS tool collects data on what the teacher is doing.
"Know Thy Impact"	2013–2014	We did several activities to discuss and study the meaning behind John Hattie's phrase "Know thy impact." We often have teachers share examples of impact in PLCs and at faculty meetings.
Feedback	2014–current	Feedback is one of the most powerful strategies. We are currently focusing on implementing meaningful and effective feedback for Admin–Teacher, Teacher–Admin, Teacher–Student, and Student–Teacher
Conference Presentation	Summer 2015	A group of teacher leaders and administrators presented at the 2015 International Visible Learning Conference last summer. Our presentation reflected our experience with implementing HYIS. Our title was "Transforming a Cruising School to an Optimal Learning Environment."

What	When	Summary
Strategies by Content	2013–current	One of the most powerful things we do on a continual basis is to break down HYIS and provide example activities of content. This allows our teachers to collaborate in PLCs and come up with activities and strategies within their specific content area.
Peer Walk-Throughs & Feedback	2014–current	We currently schedule peer walk-throughs throughout the year. This spring, we will have volunteers participate in peer feedback sessions and share the experience at a faculty meeting.

Through our work, we realize the need for continuous improvement. We know that it takes true collaboration on the part of all stakeholders. Our strategies and PLC work have impacted instruction, as we have seen gains specifically with our special education population. Through our various professional development practices, we continue to examine what is working, reflect with evidence, provide feedback, and move forward with providing the best opportunities for all students. Our school demographic and population continue to grow and change. We must constantly research intervention techniques that meet the best interest of the individual student, and it takes all of us focusing on one common mission to do that.

//

MEET, MODEL, & MOTIVATE

Meet—Many teachers are used to leaving the school building to engage in professional development. Much of that involves sit-and-get.

- Using e-mail and one faculty meeting discussion, thoroughly explain the purpose of flipped faculty meetings and why this is a viable form of professional development.

Do you believe it? If *you* believe it, they will be more likely to believe too. This may be a new concept for teachers, so the dialogue around the topic is important.

- Focus on one idea that a majority of staff is interested in and send out an article, blog, or video.

Model—It's important to help staff understand that we spend too much time on discipline and behavior issues.

- Ask the eleventh student from each class to define what good learning looks like (Visible Learning). Choosing the eleventh student in each class will ensure that you are getting a good sample of students from around the building. Get permission from parents to video students' responses.
- Show samples of the video interviews at the faculty meeting and discuss.
- Make sure that your school website, as well as the communication you send out, focuses on learning.

Motivate—Using Hattie's words, leaders need to change the dialogue.

- Keep the dialogue, or at least most of it, focused on learning.
- Through formal observations and walk-throughs, make sure that you co-construct goals around learning with staff and motivate them to find resources that will help them improve student engagement in the classroom.

DISCUSSION QUESTIONS

- How do you include all staff in professional learning?
- Are you sure that parents understand the academic changes happening in your school? Do you have dialogue with them or just send a newsletter home?
- Who is one teacher on staff that you believe has a low level of self-efficacy? What steps can you take to engage him or her? How will you help change him or her around?

Feedback (.75)

FEEDBACK IS COMPLICATED

How do we help teachers improve their teaching practices? How do we help students grow as learners? Do we know what parents really think about our school community? If they did tell us what they think, would we listen? All of these questions focus on one very important element of learning that is finally getting the credit it deserves. That crucial piece to the learning puzzle is referred to as feedback.

Useful feedback is more difficult to provide than most of us think. Once during a workshop on Hattie's feedback model, I asked the group of administrators what feedback is and is not. A sea of amazingly insightful answers flowed from one side of the room to the other, and I was a bit intimidated. My initial inner thought was "Why am I here?" The administrators had offered the same answers that were written on the upcoming slides. And then I remembered something important. The director of professional learning had sent me a copy of the formal teacher observations that every administrator had done, and 70 percent of those observations focused on praise and not feedback. It's not that the leaders didn't know what feedback was but they just hadn't yet applied their knowledge to their

It's not that the leaders didn't know what feedback was but they just hadn't yet applied their knowledge to their practice. Feedback is easy to talk about but not as easy to provide because our default reaction is to provide praise.Feedback needs to be directly related to the goals that we set with teachers otherwise it usually isn't effective at improving practice.

practice. Feedback is easy to talk about but not as easy to provide because our default reaction is to provide praise.

Feedback needs to be directly related to the goals that we set with teachers otherwise it usually isn't effective at improving practice.

This is a major reason why goal-setting is an essential aspect to formal and informal teacher evaluations. Goal-setting is even more beneficial when leaders and teachers work on it together. Prior to providing effective feedback, especially for classroom observations, leaders should reflect on where they fall in the collaborative leadership framework (see Chapter 1).

Leaders need to make sure that teachers are working on goals that they actually care about, and not on goals that they think the leader wants them to achieve. Teachers have had so many goals pushed at them over the years, especially in these days of increased accountability and mandates. Rather than working on externally imposed goals, teachers will find much more success if they work on the goals they are personally motivated to work on. Sometimes it seems as though leaders forget that teachers have advanced degrees, years of experience, and a personal commitment to improving the academic achievement of their students. It is the job of leaders to honor teachers' voices by letting them have a say in what strategies to try next. Good collaborative leaders find ways to co-construct goals with teachers. When leaders work together with teachers to set goals which revolve around student learning more than teaching, the feedback process will be much more powerful.

In *Know Thy Impact* (2012b), Hattie focuses on three questions that teachers must address when providing feedback to students. These three questions can be just as powerful for leaders to address when providing feedback to teachers.

1. *Where is the student going? Feedback that answers this question describes what success would look like in the area in which the student is working and what it would look like when he or she masters the current objective.*

2. *How is the student going? Feedback that answers this question tells where the student is on the voyage of learning. What are the student's gaps, strengths, and current achievement?*

3. *Where to next? This is particularly important. When we ask teachers to describe feedback, they typically reply that it's about constructive comments, criticisms, corrections, content, and elaboration. Students, however, value feedback that helps them know where they're supposed to go.*

By asking these questions of teachers and their practice, leaders and teachers can co-construct an effective plan and criteria for success that will lead to a better experience for students.

FEEDBACK TO MOVE LEARNING FORWARD

John Hattie's research shows that feedback, when offered around a specific goal, offers an effect size of .75. Hattie isn't the only expert to provide us with great insight into feedback. In "Seven Keys to Effective Feedback" (2012), the late Grant Wiggins wrote,

The term *feedback* is often used to describe all kinds of comments made after the fact, including advice, praise, and evaluation. But none of these are feedback, strictly speaking.

Basically, feedback is information about how we are doing in our efforts to reach a goal. I hit a tennis ball with the goal of keeping it in the court, and I see where it lands—in or out. I tell a joke with the goal of making people laugh, and I observe the audience's reaction—they laugh loudly or barely snicker. I teach a lesson with the goal of engaging students, and I see that some students have their eyes riveted on me while others are nodding off. Whether feedback is just there to be grasped or is provided by another person, helpful feedback is goal-referenced; tangible and transparent; actionable; user-friendly (specific and personalized); timely; ongoing; and consistent. (pp. 10–11)

Hattie (2012b) looks at feedback as three different levels: task, process, and self-regulation. As you can see in the table below, feedback is beneficial at every level. These levels of feedback can be applied to students, teachers, or instructional leaders.

Feedback	Student Understanding	Gradual Release of Responsibility	Example
Task	New material	I Do (Teacher to Student)	*"Khalil, I know we are just beginning our multiplication fact. You answered that 2 x 5 is 9. The answer is 10."*
Process	Some level of proficiency	We Do (Teacher and Student)	*"Khalil, I can see that you have used your knowledge of known facts to help you to this point. Can you think of another way/strategy that could help you to find the answer?"* *Can you perhaps look at the example on the board we did together and then work out your next steps?*

Feedback	Student Understanding	Gradual Release of Responsibility	Example
Self-Regulation	High level of proficiency	You Do (Student Led, Teacher Prompted)	*"Khalil, all 10 problems are correct. What is another method you could have used to answer the problems?"*

Task feedback is focused on providing the correct answer to incorrect responses. It is the type of feedback that can be given when the learning is new. Helen Butler talks about feedback as the gradual release of responsibility from teacher to student. She also sees three steps: I do, We do, You do. At the task level, the teacher shows the student how to do something (I do). After students have gained some experience, the feedback should move to the process level, which Butler explains as the teacher and student working together (We do). Process feedback focuses on the process behind the learning. In many cases, it means that teachers ask open-ended questions, focusing on the process in order to get students to understand what they should do next. Self-regulation feedback can be given when the recipient has a great deal of expertise in the area. The provider of feedback then plays the role of mentor, where the student leads and the teacher prompts (You do).

No matter how good someone may be at a task, they can always improve. Think about Michael Jordan or Wayne Gretzky. As great as they were, they always looked to become better at their sport. Even though they were the best in their sport, they still had off days where self-regulation feedback was necessary.

If you visualize the process, you can almost see the provider of feedback taking a step back through each level to give the recipient some space to figure it out on his or her own. Feedback is not about giving the answer as much as working in partnership with someone to find the best answer that will help them grow.

ONE TO GROW ON

Collaborative leaders need to have an active mind-set when doing classroom observations—either formal or informal. When I was a new teacher, my principal came in to observe me. About 10 minutes into the lesson, I saw him looking through his wallet in the back of the classroom. After the 45-minute lesson was complete, he said, "Great job" and asked me to fill out the self-reflection for the formal observation. A few days later, I received "Exceeding Expectations" in all areas of the observation, and the self-reflection I wrote was the narrative he used as his own.

Although I was happy with the results because I was a young teacher with college loans, I realize now that the observation did nothing to move my teaching forward. What he did was passive. He was not engaged with my lesson, and if it was due to my lesson not being engaging, then I should not have received the accolades I did.

As a principal, I decided things would be different. I began to break observations into three different categories: *1 to Glow On*, *1 to Grow On*, and *1 to Go On*.

1. **1 to Glow On**—This part of the feedback is something the teacher did well. It is important to focus on the strength and maybe give a few hints on how to make it better so he or she can go from good to great.

2. **1 to Grow On**—This is an area that needs improvement. For some new teachers, this may be classroom management or how to get students to work effectively in cooperative groups. It is important to suggest a follow-up such as asking the teacher to observe another teacher who excels at the given task or providing the teacher with articles that will help him or her learn different strategies to use in the classroom. One to grow on should not be seen as a weakness, but rather something the teacher isn't doing to his or her fullest potential yet.

3. **1 to Go On**—This is an area that went fairly well, and if worked on can definitely be an area of strength. Perhaps the teacher has great questioning techniques, but the instructional leader saw some students who were left out. Very likely, you noticed an area of improvement that the teacher might not be aware of. Providing resources and some insight into his or her blind spot is important.

Teachers don't want to hear all bad feedback after they put their heart into a lesson or activity. We will be much more successful if we break up our feedback into categories like one to glow on, one to grow on, and one to go on. I would love to tell you I created the concept but I didn't; but as hard as I tried to find the originators, they were nowhere to be found.

Challenge—After reflecting on past classroom observations, you realize that you have only been providing praise and not really giving teachers something they can use to grow on.

Solution—I had a moment of brutal honesty at a faculty meeting, where I told staff that I didn't do a good job of giving them feedback, and that I was worried we weren't providing it to students either. I sent them a link to an article from *Education Leadership* ahead of a faculty meeting, and we began to dive down deeper into what effective feedback looks like. It was a conversation we continued for over a year and one of the reasons why I flipped our faculty meetings.

THE MULTIPLE AVENUES OF EFFECTIVE FEEDBACK

Most of the leaders and teachers think of feedback as something we give to others. However, feedback is not only what we give but also what we receive. On any given day, students provide feedback to teachers. It isn't always verbal. Feedback can come in the form of body language or lack of engagement

> Feedback can come in the form of body language or lack of engagement in the classroom. . . . Teachers provide feedback [to administrators] by the way they sit in a faculty meeting and whether or not they are engaged with the school leader during the meeting.

in the classroom. The same can be said for the feedback between teachers and leaders. Teachers provide feedback by the way they sit in a faculty meeting and whether or not they are engaged with the school leader during the meeting. Engagement in meetings is most likely to occur when teachers and leaders co-construct the goals and the agenda. Additionally, leaders need to make sure they are spending the time creating individual relationships with teachers. A teacher who feels supported will be more engaged.

When considering feedback, leaders also need to take parents into account. As leaders and teachers, we sometimes hold up one hand, waving parents in because we want them present for open house, concerts, parent–teacher conferences, and PTA/PTO. However, we then hold up the other hand, preventing them from entering when they want to discuss a tough topic or provide us with critical feedback. Accepting, and really hearing (or seeing), the feedback given by a teacher, parent, or student is one way that leaders can ensure a more positive school climate. If teachers, parents, and students feel heard, they will be more likely to engage.

Nurturing a positive, welcoming, and engaged school climate means taking preventative measures on several levels. Stakeholders at your school should see you as someone they can approach. Otherwise, they may air their complaints on social media where it can be shared and spread very quickly. However, being open to feedback does not mean accepting abuse. If someone comes in yelling negative feedback, the leader needs to deescalate the situation immediately. Either shut the meeting down or move the person to another room to speak with him or her one on one.

Accepting negative feedback isn't easy. Leaders have to commit to really listening rather than thinking of something to say in defense. Accepting negative feedback also means not

The Do's and Don'ts of Accepting Negative Feedback	
Don't	**Do**
• React quickly	• Really listen to what the person is saying
• Take it personally . . . while they're there. Lets's face it, everyone takes feedback personally. Deal with that after they leave.	• Ask clarification questions • Repeat what they said for clarity
• Come back with a negative or defensive response	• Say, "*What I'm hearing you say is . . .*"
• Mix issues. It's easy to point out something the provider of feedback didn't do correctly at some point in their lives, but don't.	• Ask the person providing feedback for examples of what they would want you to do differently

taking it personally—easier said than done. It is not that we can't defend ourselves when feedback is harsh, but our first priority should be to try to figure out why the other person feels the way they do. Perhaps, just perhaps, that feedback will help us become better leaders. It's easy to accept positive feedback, but it's a whole lot harder to listen to the negative kind.

All in all, the best thing to do when encountering negative feedback is to learn something from it and then dust yourself off and pick yourself up knowing that a brighter day lies ahead. Following up on the feedback, even if you're on the receiving end, is really important to being able to move forward. We have to understand that in the education profession, we can learn from everything, including negative feedback.

TEACHER OBSERVATIONS: THE COLLABORATIVE APPROACH

Teacher observations are one major area where collaborative leaders give feedback. There are so many benefits to classroom observations. One significant benefit to entering classrooms

on a daily basis, especially in informal observations, is further-
ing relationships with students. You can get to know students
on a deeper level by having conversations with them during
their cooperative group time. Short observations where leaders actively engage in learning help make the formal teacher
observation process more beneficial.

Walking into the classroom also gives a collaborative
leader a sense of the classroom climate, as well as a better
understanding of what is being learned in the classroom. Being
active and observant when walking into classrooms allows
leaders to see the blind spots that teachers themselves can't
see. Constructively giving this type of feedback to teachers in
the spirit of collaboration can be very valuable to improving
the quality of student learning.

With regard to formal teacher observations, what happens when teachers and administrators do not construct goals
together? What effect does that have on the quality and usefulness of the teacher observations? Do those types of teacher
observations lead to constructive change? On my blog, *Finding
Common Ground*, I posted a link to two surveys asking about
the effectiveness of teacher observations—one for teachers and
one for administrators. The data below discusses the results of
those two surveys.

Survey Data—What do teachers and administrators say about the effectiveness of teacher observations?

Teachers

Unfortunately, there is often a disconnect between teachers and
leaders when it comes to observations. In a small scale survey
involving over two hundred teachers from North America, most
responded that observations were not beneficial to them (*Finding
Common Ground* blog). The respondents were evenly distributed
between elementary, middle, and secondary teachers.

When asked if the goals for the observation were co-
constructed between leaders and teachers, 77 percent of the

teachers answered no. When respondents were asked whether observations were beneficial to them as teachers, 9 percent of teachers said yes, 44 percent said no, and 46 percent said sometimes. Below are some of the open-ended responses given.

Are observations beneficial to you as a teacher?

- My administrator does not know how to evaluate good or bad teaching and therefore there is no constructive feedback.
- It is a hindrance in my confidence.
- The process is just a numbers game; if you can play it, you're OK.
- I ask for my principal to "just walk in" so I can find out what I'm doing well and what I need to work on during a typical day. Many times the observation is scheduled and the postobservation is just me trying to defend how I'm reaching all of the Danielson points.
- I feel I know more than the principal. This principal has not taught this level. I do not learn anything from the postobservation conversation.
- The evaluation tool is subjective and my data show that my students have grown. My principal uses the evaluation tool as a means to break teachers. I have witnessed this process at my school over the past three years.
- In the charter school where I worked previously, we "Over observed" and they would find at least one thing I did wrong in each obs. In my new public school, we are observed the state minimum. For the most part, the conference is all lollipops and lullabies. What I used to hate about my old school, I now miss here. Telling me I am doing great and keep up the good work does little to help me grow as an educator. It is great to be appreciated but I would prefer a happy medium that gives me something to take away and work for or toward. During one observation this year, my vice principal left her running thoughts she had recorded on her notes on the sheet that I saw. I LOVED it. Lots of good feedback but she also spoke about what she wished I had done. I have asked her to leave those notes on my observation forms from now on.
- I like to know where I can improve my teaching.

(Continued)

(Continued)

- NO—Because my administrator has already made up her mind before having a conversation with me as to what she will be looking at
- The only times I am observed are my formal observations.

What is the best advice you have received from your school leaders?

- I haven't. There is such a "caughtya" attitude that absolutely nothing she says helps me.
- The best information I have learned regarding instruction has come from other teachers and peer administrators.
- Nothing. The observation is done because it is a requirement. If you are on the observer's good side, you are stellar. If you aren't, the observation can be used to bury you. That's the sad reality.
- It is one sided, usually, especially in my case. The Admin has no experience with special needs students, planning for them, and how and why things are done! It's dehumanizing, humiliating, and destructive! Nothing positive or constructive about that!!!!
- Nothing
- I have yet to discuss with my administrator anything at all concerning the observations. I presume the observations are merely checked off his list as items completed.
- Suggestions on what classes or training I need for a specific problem in my class.
- That it is okay to not follow the lesson plan. In my lesson write-up, I had planned to do a particular activity but it was clear that my students were not ready for the next step. I needed to step back and reteach a strategy before moving on. Normally, I would have done that right then and there but I didn't because I wrote a lesson plan for the formal observation and I wanted to stick to it. In the end, I should have done what I would have normally done but I didn't. My principal made sure that I understood that adjusting is what good teachers do and not to focus on the lesson plan but on the students. And now I wish I would have just taught how I would have normally taught.

- Steps to take to encourage 3rd graders to not only have critical thinking conversations in answers to questions that I pose, but to encourage/teach them to ask those critical thinking questions and moderate the discussion between themselves.
- I can't think of anything in recent years. As a first year teacher, I would receive constructive feedback for improvement in various areas, but nothing in recent years. Sad really.
- How to play the game.
- To state my learning goals concretely to students.
- Nothing . . . Typically the principal does not offer any on-the-spot solutions or feedback other than numbers. The usual response to areas that need work is to let them know how they can help.
- Sometimes I will receive suggestions for improvement. Rare, but helpful.
- That they think I'm generally a good teacher and that I have a good relationship with my students.
- How to meet his standards for what he wants to see in a class-room—and how much he isn't aware of the needs of the students I'm teaching. For example, I was written up negatively about two students who had on hats/earphones when he came in—this indicated that I wasn't enforcing school rules—one of the two was suspended and expelled the next week, and the other was a chronically noncompliant student who subsequently cut class for a week and was just suspended for drug use on campus. So now I've started having conversations with my noncompliant students to let them know that I'm being held accountable for their decisions to sneak the hat and earphones back on after I've already reviewed the rules at the start of class.
- Areas of strength, areas for growth.
- Who to go to, to see a sample of exactly how she wanted our "self-reflection record" to look. :((I resigned this year.)
- To formulate better questions to promote learning
- I have learned to notice certain things about myself during lessons and new techniques to improve a lesson
- no advice, only criticism
- Twenty years ago, the assistant principal praised me for taking a risk and intentionally inviting her to observe on a day when I was trying a new lesson.

Leaders often point out that many teachers don't want to be observed, therefore they react defensively. This is evident from some of the responses above. However, it is very likely that teachers would be more open to the observation process if they enjoyed a supportive school climate and they were given the opportunity to co-construct the goal to be worked on with the school leader. If teachers in your school gave you feedback similar to that included above, what action steps would you take to improve the collaborative climate in your school?

What Is a Good Goal?

If the particular school has a buildingwide goal around learning, then a teacher's goal should be able to fit into that overall building goal.

If a particular school has a nonspecific goal like "All Students Can Learn," then the teacher has a little more flexibility about co-creating a goal with the school leader; but it should still focus on student learning.

Teacher goals, as well as school leader goals, should focus on student learning. This may sound like common sense, but there are many instances where a teacher's goal is to be on time to school, to not use as many worksheets, or to create more opportunities for center-based learning. The reality is that these may be important, but we need to get to the heart of how all of these affect student learning. We must be clear and use concise language that provide us with a measurable goal that can include all students.

Administrators

In addition to wanting to gather data on how teachers felt about the usefulness of observations, I also wanted to collect data separately to see if leaders felt that the feedback they gave was beneficial to teachers. In a survey tailored to school leaders, we received fifty-eight responses.

Grade level

- 58% elementary-level school leaders
- 18% middle-level school leaders
- 24% high school-level school leaders

Years of experience

- 35%, 5 years or less
- 31%, 6–10 years
- 10%, 10–15 years
- 24%, 16 years or more

School administrator respondents came from an even mix of rural, suburban, and urban schools. Fifty percent had assistant principals to help with school duties, 50 percent were without an assistant principal. There was an even split between school leaders who had 500 students or less, and 500 students or more in their school population. Although this is a small sample compared to that of the teachers I had surveyed, the information was still very useful.

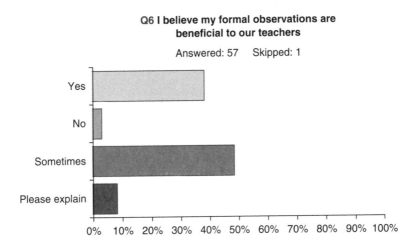

Q6 I believe my formal observations are beneficial to our teachers

Answered: 57   Skipped: 1

Very few of the school leaders believed that their observations were not beneficial, but almost 50 percent of the school leader respondents felt that their observations were beneficial only sometimes. Out of the fifty-eight, five respondents gave more in-depth answers to the following prompt:

I believe my formal observations are beneficial to our teachers.

- The new evaluation system prohibits the time needed to give/get meaningful feedback.
- Some teachers don't want to learn from them.
- We focus on specific predetermined areas in the observation and there are criteria to be addressed about various expectations re: work outside of the classroom so the reporting is quite comprehensive.
- It all depends on the attitude of the observed teacher to the feedback.
- I believe they are as valuable as a teacher is willing to reflect, accept feedback, listen to positive observations, and accept advice and recommendations.

When asked whether they believed that their feedback focused on student learning, close to 60 percent of school leaders answered yes, while close to 40 percent answered sometimes.

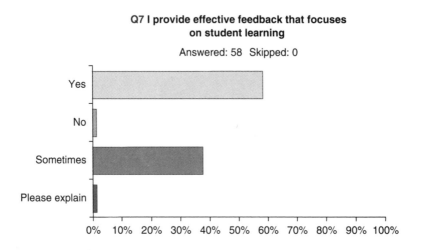

Q7 I provide effective feedback that focuses on student learning

Answered: 58   Skipped: 0

When asked what the biggest obstacle was to the observation process, overwhelmingly, *time* was seen as the culprit to the process, although almost half of the respondents had assistant principals.

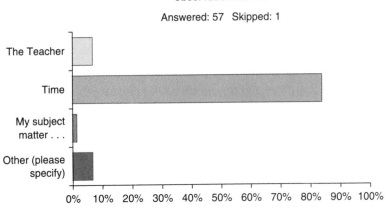

Q8 The biggest obstacle to formal observations is . . .

Answered: 57 Skipped: 1

These results hint at a much larger issue, which is that there is a disconnect between principals who believe that they offer effective feedback to teachers and teachers' written responses indicate that feedback is not effective.

One area where principals can work on being more effective is in the formal conversations that follow teacher observations. Rather than one-sided monologues, leaders should work toward a mutually respectful dialogue between two professionals. Deidre M. Le Fevre and Viviane Robinson (2014) found,

> Overall, principals demonstrated consistently low to moderate levels of skill across the two conversations. Typically, principals were more skilled in advocating their own position than in deeply inquiring into and checking their understanding of the views of the parent or teacher. (p. 1)

This is where the positions of the bystander, negotiator, and regulator surface quite a bit. A bystander will easily accept the conversation and not add any depth to it, whereas the negotiator will manipulate his or her way through the conversation in order to bring the other professional to the decision the negotiator wants. And when it comes to the regulator, he or she shuts down the conversation and tells the other professionals where they went wrong. What observations need are collaborative leaders who will learn from the other professional as the dialogue goes on.

The following blog post offers some tips on how school leaders can offer beneficial feedback to teachers.

Leaders: Are Your Teacher Observations Active or Passive?

By Peter DeWitt

March 29, 2015

blogs.edweek.org

If you were ever a teacher, you remember the teacher observation process. Perhaps one was announced, which means you went through the goal-setting process, had the observation that lasted around 45 minutes, and then met with the principal in his or her office to have the formal conversation after the observation.

Many times those observations resulted in receiving very little feedback.

Unannounced observations have become popular too. It's not about the "gotcha" but about observing teachers and students in their natural elements. Principals walk in and stay for some length of time, and then the teacher receives an evaluation of what the principal saw. In best case scenarios, teachers and principals meet to "discuss" the observation . . . in the principal's office, but in the worst case scenarios, teachers receive an observation form without a conversation.

Whether it was announced or unannounced, teachers are more relieved to have it over.

The importance of teacher observations has increased a great deal over the years due to accountability measures. Unfortunately, just because observations are tied to point scales doesn't mean they provide any more feedback to teachers. It is often seen as a process to get done . . . instead of a process to get done right.

And when I say "right," I do not mean a heavy-handed, top-down observation that focus on weaknesses without acknowledging strengths; and I also do not mean observations that result in great praise even though the principal may not have been paying attention.

Are your observations worthwhile?

Many times, I have been in rooms with teachers who acknowledge that their observations haven't resulted in new learning. The reasons span from the idea that the principal has never taught that particular subject so can't provide any true insight (which is false by the way) to the principal is super busy and can't possibly provide effective observations, which is sometimes due to nonsensical accountability measures or bad time management.

When it comes to teacher observations, there have historically been two types. One is passive and the other is active. We know what passive looks like. The teacher puts on all the pomp and circumstance while the principal sits in the back and takes notes for 45 minutes. When the alarm goes off in the principal's head, he or she gets up and moves on to another observation or back to his or her office.

The more effective way to go through the observation process is by being an active observer. Principals need to approach teacher observations like an instructional coach (IC). Why? Because instructional coaches approach the process more differently than principals do. Instructional coaching expert Jim Knight (2008) says,

> ICs partner with teachers to help them incorporate research-based instructional practices into their teaching. They are skilled communicators, or relationship builders, with a repertoire of excellent communication skills that enable them to empathize, listen, and build trusting relationships. ICs also encourage and support teachers' reflection about their classroom practices. Thus, they must be skilled at unpacking their collaborating teachers' professional goals so that they can help them create a plan for realizing those goals, all with a focus on improving instruction. (p. 30)

(Continued)

(Continued)

> [Instructional Coaches] encourage and support teachers' reflection about their classroom practices. Thus, they must be skilled at unpacking their collaborating teachers' professional goals so that they can help them create a plan for realizing those goals, all with a focus on improving instruction. (Jim Knight, 2008)

THAT is how principals should approach the process. Teachers should be able to learn what they do well, what needs some tweaking, and what needs improving. The observation process should be structured like instructional coaches do it so that the focus is on providing effective feedback to bring learning forward.

Instructional coaches and teachers agree on a unified goal and have conversations around what learning should look like. ICs find resources, have conversations that don't focus on evaluation, and are there to teach, coach, and mentor teachers, but they also are learning through the process and get to stretch their own thinking as well.

Instructional coaching isn't just about the teacher learning from the coach; it is also about the coach learning from the teacher, which is what the observation process should be for principals. We should approach every single observation as if it will provide us something to learn from, and not merely something to get through.

School climate

Principals can't change the process overnight. It takes a positive and inclusive school climate where risks are respected and not frowned upon. Providing effective feedback is something that needs to be discussed at faculty meetings so all stakeholders understand what it looks like, that sometimes it doesn't feel good because it's hard to hear, and that the point of feedback is to improve learning.

Too many of us have criticized our own principals for providing observations that resulted in too little learning and a whole lot of pomp and circumstance. We need to be different, so that our teachers don't get into a closed room and say they learn very little from our observation process.

Being an active observer and approaching observations like an instructional coach may help knock down some of those old walls that have stood too long between the roles we play in school. Approaching observations like an IC means that there is more to the process than two observations a year. It is about co-constructing an aspiration, understanding where student learning fits into that observation, and having multiple conversations throughout the year.

Things to consider:

- Have observation meetings in the teacher's classroom and not the principal's office.
- What is your aspiration for the school? Do the teachers know it? Do the students? What about the parents?
- Use the faculty meeting as a place to discuss observations and feedback and put a focus on learning every time you meet with teachers.
- You may know what feedback is – but are you applying it with teachers?
- Before and after the observation, are you asking questions or are you doing a majority of the talking?

One path to better classroom observations would be for school leaders and teachers to engage in collaborative conversations about what works in classrooms, what is happening in the classrooms for those particular teachers, and how they can work together (teacher and administrator) to create professional development opportunities that would improve the quality of student learning in that classroom and the school.

Co-constructed goals are filled with *simplexity*, a word coined by Michael Fullan. According to Fullan and Quinn (2015), simplexity is where leaders

Take a difficult problem and identify a small number of key factors—this is the simple part. And then you make these factors gel under the reality of action with its pressures, politics, and personalities in the situation—this is the complex part. (p. 127)

What needs to happen during a teacher observation is that a leader and teacher identify an individual goal together. The goal, to take from the work of Jim Knight, should focus on student learning or teacher instruction, and in the best case scenario, should be chosen by the teacher and then improved through the conversation with the leader. Once that goal has been defined, the leader enters into the classroom to complete an evidence-based observation where he or she provides evidence and feedback around the identified goal. Ask "Did the teachers meet the goal?" and "What evidence can I provide the teachers to help them understand that they did or did not meet the goal?" Provide feedback in the postobservation conversation, co-construct a plan of action with the teacher to address how things can be improved, and then, and this is crucial, go back for a second look after a specified amount of time to see if the teacher reached the goal.

Collaborative Leaders

Co-construct a goal prior to the formal observation. It will provide you with something to look for when observing and will make it easier to provide effective feedback to teachers. At the end of the postconversation after the observation is completed, make sure you ask the teacher if there was something they would have wished you had seen when observing.

For those with large buildings and multiple assistant principals: Divide teachers up by grade levels or teams so that observations are not seen as something to just get done. Sometimes observations are approached in a triage method because there are so many to accomplish. Dividing observations among assistant principals may "lessen the load" and provide more time for offering effective feedback.

Suggestion: If you are a part of an administrative team in your school, set aside some time to meet with the administrative team and discuss the observations that were completed. Discuss what each administrator saw in the lesson, what kind of learning took place, who has strengths that need to be shared among staff (collective teacher efficacy), and who needs some special coaching in order to improve.

In Jim Knight's instructional coaching work (2007), he established a coaching cycle where a teacher and coach establish a goal, engage in the learning around the goal (e.g., find resources, coteach, model lessons, etc.) and then focus on how to improve around that goal.

Taking Knight's nonevaluative instructional coaching cycle and adapting it to the evaluative leadership level, the steps should include the following:

- co-constructing a goal,
- observing (collecting evidence) around the goal to provide effective feedback,
- engaging in a postobservation meeting providing the feedback and having authentic dialogue around what needs to happen next in order to improve,
- teacher and leader finding resources to assist in the improvement, and
- leaders going back into the classroom to collect evidence around the improvement.

**Cycle of Collaborative
Teacher Leadership**

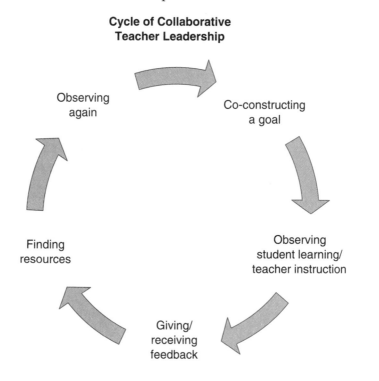

Observing again

Co-constructing a goal

Finding resources

Observing student learning/ teacher instruction

Giving/ receiving feedback

Feedback is one of the most important areas of teaching and leading. Students can learn at deeper levels when teachers provide them with effective feedback. Additionally, teachers can learn at deeper levels when leaders provide them with effective feedback. In addition to the type of feedback that improves student learning and teacher practice is the type of feedback administrators receive from parents and community members. Sometimes this feedback is negative. Responding to negative feedback is complicated because leaders have to try to understand where the individual person is coming from when they are providing feedback. Whether feedback is given to teachers and students or received from the school community, collaborative leaders should consider giving feedback and responding to feedback in ways that foster a positive school climate and create a community of learners.

//

School Story—A New Collaboration

by Lisa Meade, Principal of Corinth Middle School

Corinth, NY

Taking over as a school principal at the start of the 2012–2013 school year after the previous leader passed away from a lung transplant failure was not easy. Every position comes with challenges, but those shoes of a beloved leader who had been in the role for sixteen years were hard to fill. There had been two interims while he was in the hospital battling his illness, which provided the building with instability after so many years of stability.

What made it more of a challenge was that I was asked to be the middle school principal and Director of Special Education, which was one full-time job for two full-time positions. Coming from the position of Director of K–12 Student Services was an area of comfort, but the building leader role was outside my comfort zone.

The middle school was notified at the end of the school year in June 2012 that I would be taking over the reins in the fall. The teachers and staff had spent more than a year working hard to keep the building afloat, but now they found themselves in the position of having absolutely no say in who would become their leader. It was a matter of staff reassignment in the district and I campaigned hard with my superintendent to be at the middle school. I hadn't had much experience at this level but something told me that was where I needed, and very much wanted, to be.

As a new leader, I knew there were a variety of areas that could be tackled first: observations, feedback, instruction, planning, culture, discipline, for example. Although this list was long, culture stood out as our first priority. Culture were those norms, areas of social-emotional focus and common language that we could establish as a staff, and climate was how the students, parents, and teachers would feel about the culture we set.

As I reflect on the last three years, I think there are some key action steps that helped us improve our building's culture.

Involve building leadership team—As soon as I was notified of the appointment, I immediately met with the team leaders in the building to gauge their sense of priorities in the building. I asked for honest feedback and they provided it. My leadership team knows their role is to canvass their teams and bring me back any feedback, negative or positive. We can't move forward if we ignore the white elephants.

Develop a process for student behavior—The commitment to implement Positive Behavioral Interventions and Supports (PBIS) was made prior to my appointment, and I was more than happy to help see that commitment through. This involved meetings and work over the summer preparing materials for teachers that spoke to teacher and student expectations. The work gave us clear information about what was teacher managed and what was office managed. We provided some professional development and information to our staff in the beginning of the new school year and appointed a PBIS team to help steer the work in our building. During the first two or three days each year, we shared this information explicitly with our students. Entire days were devoted to teaching expectations and celebrating student ideas around PBIS.

Being more than visible—Every arrival and dismissal is a time to connect with students. High fives and "good mornings" matter even when their faces may pretend otherwise. Walking the halls during class transitions became another time to make connections with a student. I moved from having lunch in my office to eating in the cafeteria with students. It's always random because I sit down at a table and wait for students to approach me. They always do.

At first, they were surprised that their principal would even eat lunch but that wore off eventually. As DeWitt says, we need to be more than visible. We need to visit classrooms as much as possible and sit with students to engage with them. Ask them to explain the work to you. It matters.

Listening to their formal and informal feedback— When I talk with students, I ask them about school and their learning. What are you learning about? Why is it important? What do you think about this? There have also been formal opportunities to gather student feedback through student surveys and student roundtables.

Celebrate—Send positive handwritten notes home to parents about their students. Send a lot of them! Use Twitter, Facebook, and blogging as a way to share images and thoughts about students in our school.

//

MEET, MODEL, & MOTIVATE

Meet

- Not everyone understands what feedback is and is not. At a faculty meeting, use John Hattie's article in *Educational Leadership* about the levels of effective feedback.
- Understand that parents have a different perspective on education based on the experiences they had as a

student and not just the experiences they have as a parent. Listen to the feedback they may provide.

Model

- Make an effort to provide one piece of effective feedback on each teacher observation that you complete. Use one to glow on, one to grow on, and one to go on.
- When talking with parents, teachers, or students, model what it means to listen to feedback, even if that feedback is critical. Don't complain about the parents after they leave you with negative feedback because that will model to teachers and staff that you do not value honest feedback. Instead, ask deeper questions like "Why does/did he or she feel that way?"

Motivate

- Use feedback surveys from parents, teachers, or students to make one change in the school. Just focus on one area to change based on the feedback that was provided. Think . . . short term wins.

DISCUSSION QUESTIONS

- Do you provide effective feedback to staff and students? How do you know?
- How do you ensure that the formal observation process will end in new learning for both you and the teacher being observed?
- Do you talk with a wide range of students during an observation to make sure that they are all learning?
- When you receive negative feedback from a stakeholder, what do you do with it? How do you move forward?

7

Family Engagement (.49)

Too many times family engagement means to educators that parents should support what the teachers want. This is very one sided. Family engagement shouldn't just be about making sure that the needs of the school are met. Family engagement is about a collaborative relationship between staff and parents with the students at the center.

We know from reports like "A New Wave of Evidence" (Henderson & Mapp, 2002) from the National Center for Family and Community Connections with Schools that "When schools, families, and community groups work together to support learning, children tend to do better in school, stay in school longer, and like school more" (p. 7).

> Family engagement is about a collaborative relationship between staff and parents with the students at the center.

The report goes on to say,

> When parents talk to their children about school, expect them to do well, help them plan for college, and make sure that out-of-school activities are constructive, their children do better in school. When schools engage families in ways that are linked to improving learning, students make greater gains. When schools build partnerships with families that respond to their concerns and honor their contributions, they are successful in sustaining connections that are aimed at improving student achievement. And when families and communities organize to hold poorly performing schools accountable, studies suggest that school districts make positive changes in policy, practice, and resources. (p. 8).

Parents are vitally important to the school community. In a meta-analysis for the Harvard Family Research Project, William H. Jeyens found that parental involvement, which I am replacing with family engagement, had a high effect size. Jeyens (2005) writes,

> For the overall population of students, on average, the achievement scores of children with highly involved parents was higher than children with less involved parents. This academic advantage for those parents who were highly involved in their education averaged about .5 to .6 of a standard deviation for overall educational outcomes, grades, and academic achievement. In other words, the academic achievement score distribution or range of scores for children whose parents were highly involved in their education was substantially higher than that of their counterparts whose parents were less involved. (p. 1)

Jeyens found that parental expectations were typically higher where the largest effect sizes emerged. Parents with high expectations for their children's academic achievement had children who achieved at higher levels than parents who had low expectations or none at all. This finding corroborates that of John Hattie's work around student expectations of themselves and teachers' expectations of students.

It's very difficult to create and maintain positive relationships with parents unless collaborative leaders understand how to meet parents where they are and find ways to motivate them to want to be involved, which also means understanding the different ways families are involved in the lives of their children.

WHY FAMILY ENGAGEMENT IS DIFFICULT

In some schools, certain families are valued more than others. Not all teachers and leaders appreciate the diverse family dynamics that enter into school each year. Diversity in our student population keeps increasing each year. It's not something that is going away. According to the US Census Bureau (Lofquist, 2011), there were 594,000 same-sex couples living together in 2010 (p. 2). The same census showed that 4.2 million households in the United States had biracial couples (Saulney, 2011). Additionally, the American Association of Retired Persons (AARP) reports that over 5.8 million children are living with their grandparents. In addition to the physical makeup of families, there exists diversity in parenting styles. Not all parents parent the same way, and leaders and teachers have to understand that just because a parenting style looks different doesn't mean it's wrong. Family dynamics in this country are always changing; it us up to us as educators to change with them.

One change we can make toward a more positive and welcoming school climate is to stop thinking of these issues as parental involvement and start moving toward family engagement. This is not in an effort to be more politically correct, but is an effort to have a more holistic focus on the way we look at students who come from homes that seem different. Family engagement is about understanding that some students live with parents, grandparents, uncles, or aunts, and that does not have to result in a sad commentary about a new family structure. Collaborative leaders strive to understand the family dynamics of students and serve as mediators between parents or guardians and teachers.

Collaborative leadership is about welcoming families into school, even if they may be there to tell the principal something he or she doesn't want to hear. It's part of the partnership approach to leading. Just like the emotional bank account (Covey, 1989) philosophy that I discussed in Chapter 3, collaborative leaders understand that they need to build relationships with parents. Steven Constantino (2015) writes,

> Some families hold the perception that they do not have easy or thorough access to information about school. They believe that teachers blame them when their children have issues in school and feel unwelcome to engage. These same families believe that teachers only share negative information and that teachers wait until things are at a boiling point before communicating with the family. (p. 29)

Collaborative leadership is about addressing these types of concerns from families in order to move past the philosophy of the old days when school was considered the teacher's domain and the home was the domain of the parents.

Families need to be in the know. When schools make changes, they need to make sure they articulate that to parents. Instead of just focusing on how families can support schools, schools have to make sure they are focusing on how schools can support parents by communicating about their child's learning.

Letting Parents in on the Secret of School

by Peter DeWitt

February 22, 2015

blogs.edweek.org

Let's get two of the most common obstacles out of the way first . . .

Some parents don't want to engage—Perhaps, they had a tough school experience when they were growing up. Maybe, they feel intimidated that we engage in educational talk and they don't always know the acronyms. What if we tried just one more conversation? What if we channeled Stephen Covey and tried to understand a little bit more?

Some treat us like childcare—This absolutely happens but perhaps they are just recycling the same role they lived with their own parents. Maybe they don't see the importance of education, or they don't show it, because they lost hope along the way.

School staff have always had an interesting relationship with parents. We can't love all parents, right? BUT, there have been times when school teachers and leaders seem to hold up one hand inviting parents into the school for open house, parent–teacher conferences, concerts, and PTA nights, but hold the other hand up when a parent has a difficult topic they would like to have a conversation about.

Most teachers and parents have a positive relationship, and we need to find innovative ways to keep fostering that. Flipping leadership and holding stakeholder meetings are a couple of ways to do that. But we also have parents who are disengaged and we need to do something about that. Too many walk away feeling as though we don't care about them or their children.

When we send mixed messages, we are often missing a great opportunity.

Popular Parents

We can deny that this happens but throughout schools we have parents who are popular, or at least that is the way other parents see them. Let's face it, when it comes to parents who support us on an ongoing basis, or those who make our lives easier, we treat them differently.

When I was a principal, I always had an awesome PTA. We were small but mighty. Unfortunately, some parents wouldn't attend the meetings because we seemed like a closed group. One inside joke or the way the parents who consistently attended sat with each other . . . we sent a message that we were an elite group who didn't want help.

It's not who we were but that is what parents thought. Like a high school clique, the parents who were always able to attend events, or those who strived extra hard to attend, were seen as the parents who were popular. It took a lot of work to change that perception.

It meant that I had to spend extra time at bus arrival to go out of my way to talk with parents I didn't know well. It meant that Donna, our school secretary, had to go the extra mile to make sure those parents who were not regular visitors felt welcome in the school. It means that the great principals and teachers I know through my Twitter professional learning network (PLN) have to put in extra effort to engage, which they do on a daily basis, with those parents who don't seem to want to engage.

It means that we have to suspend judgment on the parents who don't engage like we want to because we don't always know what they have going on at home.

The Secret of School

School leaders and teachers do their best to engage parents in the fun events or the ones that focus on report cards and grades like parent-teacher conferences. But we don't always engage parents when it comes to those things that focus on learning. It's a balance because we don't want to always use educational language, but we also don't want to patronize them by using noneducational language either.

The bottom line is that when we are initiating changes within our classrooms and schools, we have to make sure we don't leave parents out of the equation. For example, a few of us who train schools around the use of John Hattie's Visible Learning (VL) were working with a great group of educators from Kentucky. As we met in a convention center in Bowling Green, we began having dialogue around a few important elements of VL.

As we discussed how to move forward, we needed to focus on how important parents were to the process. For example, when it comes to the use of learning intentions and success criteria, it's important that parents know what those look like in order to support the work at home.

If schools engage in instructional coaching (IC), it's important that parents know what that looks like. How great would it be for parents

(Continued)

(Continued)

to know that teachers are really opening up their practices in the classroom and working in collaboration with other professionals? Explaining IC would help parents understand how school has changed and that teachers are always working to improve practice.

We are fighting a media that seems to focus on how lazy we are when that couldn't be any further from the truth!

Starr Sackstein and Mark Barnes focus on throwing out grades in an effort to really concentrate on providing effective feedback to students. Effective feedback focuses on growth and not just achievement. Parents need to understand why grades are disappearing in these classrooms. They need to know what effective feedback looks like and why providing feedback is more important than grades.

My friend Christina Luce, a third-grade teacher in Liverpool, New York, has a Twitter page and she tweets out pictures of her students learning throughout the day. The parents in the classroom know what is going on and are better able to talk about learning with their children at the dinner table.

Like Christina Luce, we need to let parents in on the secret of school.

In the End

We assume there are topics that parents don't need to know about when we engage in new initiatives or changes, when the reality is that they are the very topics that parents need to know about. They can be our biggest advocates with their very own children, and letting them in on the secret of school will help them understand that some of what we do may have changed from when they were students.

When discussing instructional topics with families, it's important to maintain clarity without using too much educational jargon and acronyms.

School leaders and teachers need to let families know what is happening in the classroom, while making sure they don't turn families off by using educationalese. How often have we been a part of special education meetings where the district sends in twelve professionals, but only one parent is present?

If I had to go to a doctor's appointment and meet alone with twelve doctors, I would be very intimidated. If I had to go to where I get my car serviced and meet with twelve mechanics, I would be even more intimidated. Collaborative leadership is about being sensitive to how we communicate with families' needs without talking down to them.

The National PTA developed six standards for schools to keep in mind when working with parents and families.

Standard 1: Welcoming all families into the school community

Standard 2: Communicating effectively

Standard 3: Supporting student success

Standard 4: Speaking up for every child

Standard 5: Sharing power

Standard 6: Collaborating with community

How We Communicate With Parents

One night, a friend of mine messaged me asking for help with his second-grade granddaughter's math homework. He was frustrated and said how much he hated the Common Core. I wondered if Chris hated the Common Core, what it represented, and the homework that his granddaughter was doing, or was he frustrated because no one took the time to explain the new problem-solving techniques to him? Chris's reaction to the Common Core (CCSS) was replicated by thousands of other families in New York State. Schools didn't take the time to explain the CCSS to families and therefore the families placed their frustrations on the curriculum. Families heard many others having the same issues so they concluded that the whole thing was a waste of time.

Do you think you're out of the woods because the CCSS implementation went well in your district? Think again. Take the CCSS out of the equation and think of other initiatives that have failed in your school. We can learn a lot from failure. Might those initiatives have succeeded if the school had made more of an effort to explain the initiative to parents in ways they could readily understand? Would it have helped to get parents' support for the initiative early on? Engaging parents isn't just about sending colorful newsletters home that only give dates and times instead of real information about learning. Being a collaborative leader involves including parents as important contributors toward the goal of student learning by providing families with information about aspirations, curriculum initiatives, and the importance of student voice. Collaborative leaders can also welcome families in by sharing all of the great ways that the school is working with the community at large. As a principal, one of the ways that I engaged families was by flipping family communications.

FLIPPING FAMILY COMMUNICATIONS

Flipped faculty meetings, as explained in Chapter 5, are intended to help staff explore a particular topic in depth. After seeing the usefulness of flipping faculty meetings, I decided to flip some of the communication I had with families as well. I was concerned that, as with the staff, my communication with families might be overly focused on dates and rather than topics of substance. There are so many changes happening in education, some good and some bad. Flipping the communication offers an opportunity to let families know what is going on.

In 2012, as I was preparing for open house, I sent parents a video that focused on some of the important things they needed to know about the school year, such as where to park during events, bus arrival and dismissal, PTA, the Common Core, and the Dignity for All Students Act (anti-bullying legislation). I recorded myself talking through the topics, which included a few pictures, and explained what flipped communication meant.

After I sent the video link to parents and guardians through our family portal, I was surprised when I received a great deal of positive feedback. Why? There were many parents and guardians who could not volunteer at school because they worked, and they wanted and needed to know what was going on. I checked out the views of the video and it was in the hundreds.

The night of open house, there was standing room only in the gymnasium, which wasn't out of the ordinary. However, what was unusual was that because of the information provided on the video, we were able to have a robust discussion about the Common Core and bullying. We talked about what bullying is and what it is not. It was a powerful discussion and I heard from many parents later who said that they loved the flipped approach. Below is a list of some other options principals can consider for flipping communication with parents.

Options for Flipping Communication With Parents

PTA—Prior to PTA meetings, send out information for the meeting and some possible topics to cover. If the topics are intriguing enough, it might encourage more parents to show up at the meeting.

Special events—Use the flipped model to send a quick 5-minute video in preparation for school events to explain why you are doing what you are doing. Possibilities include No Testing Week, Grandparents and Special Person's Day, or No Name-Calling Week.

State assessments—Sometimes families do not understand the importance of getting their children to school on time for state assessments or the length of the exam. You can improve parent cooperation (and therefore test scores) by sending a presentation explaining how long the exam takes, in both minutes and number of days, and the importance of their children's involvement.

(Continued)

(Continued)

Any Educational Issue—The reality is that parents and guardians need to know what is happening in education. Whether it's a simple tutorial on the Common Core State Standards or new anti-bullying legislation like the Dignity for All Students Act in New York State or The FAIR Education Act in California, or why we use interactive whiteboards in the classroom, your school initiatives will enjoy more success if you make an effort to get parents' support. You can do this by sending them the information they need in an easy-to-digest format employing the flipped model.

> With smartphones and all of the new technological tools at our disposal, we have more and more ways to communicate with parents and guardians, and they with us. Whether it's face-to-face conversations, e-mails, or newsletters, every communication we have with families is important because we represent our school and district through our actions and words.

With smartphones and all of the new technological tools at our disposal, we have more and more ways to communicate with parents and guardians, and they with us. Whether it's face-to-face conversations, e-mails, or newsletters, every communication we have with families is important because we represent our school and district through our actions and words. Families deserve to see the tools and resources that we use with their children. Working those tools into our communication with parents and guardians is the best way to do that. Flipping family communication is just one example of how we can share one of our instructional practices. Flipping is not meant to take the place of other forms of communication with parents, but to enhance the other forms of communication already in use.

THE PARTNERSHIP APPROACH

Just like with teachers, collaborative leaders need to work in partnership with parents. The 7 Partnership Principles developed by Jim Knight are a useful guide for inviting parents to be partners in the school.

The Principles of Partnership (Knight, 2011)

Equality—It's not top down. All stakeholders are equal. Collaborative leaders understand how to make all parents and guardians feel as though they are equals when they walk into the school. As soon as parents feel that the school leader is taking an authoritarian stance, they will tune out, curse out, or run out.

- Meet with parent or guardian in the library instead of the office.
- If leaders meet parents in the office because of privacy, at least sit at a table and not behind a desk.

Choice—Have an open door policy at the school. Families should know they are welcome regardless of their reasons for being there.

- Offer coffee-talk times with families once a month so they can come in and discuss issues with other families.
- If parents and guardians have an issue, don't make them wait if they don't have to. You may not have all the answers at the time, but you can at least offer them your time and an open ear.

Voice—Just like students, teachers, and school leaders, families deserve to have a voice in the school community.

- If possible, invite a couple of parents or guardians, and not just the ones who always agree with you, to be a part of your Principals Advisory Council (PAC) or your stakeholder group.
- Flip your communication and give them the opportunity to respond back. This may be as simple as providing your e-mail address in every communication.

- Create a survey to do every month or a couple of times a year. Be sure to change what you can based on the survey feedback and provide an explanation for the things you cannot change.

Reflection—Provide parents and guardians with prompts that offer reflection time. For example, ask a question at the end of PTA meeting about curriculum that parents and guardians can reflect on and respond to at the next meeting.

- Send report cards home well before parent–teacher conferences so parents can reflect on the report card and arrive with questions. Don't give the report card 5 minutes before the meeting and then expect questions.
- Add a question of the month to the newsletter to make it a bit more engaging.

Dialogue—Every conversation leaders have with families contributes to (or detracts from) the emotional bank account. Speak less and listen more. Engage in authentic dialogue with parents or guardians.

- Don't interrupt. Listen—really listen to what they are saying.

Praxis—Offer parents the opportunity to run PTA meetings or stakeholder meetings where they can ask questions and put their knowledge into practice. If you want to engage families in dialogue about standards and curriculum, offer nights during the year when parents can come to school to work on a particular curriculum assignment with their children. For example:

- Math Night
- STEM Night
- Science Fair
- Discovery Day
- Learning Night—Let's put the focus on learning

Reciprocity—Everyone should be taking the time to learn from one another. Knight says, "We should expect to get as much as we give." I had a principal who said that parents were sending the best children they have every day, and we should respect that. Give parents and guardians the respect they deserve, regardless of who they are and what they do, and they will give it to you.

I have been a part of conversations where teachers or leaders don't treat parents well, and vice versa. I once came upon a conversation between two teachers in the faculty room and one was not being kind regarding a parent. The only thing I said is that if they didn't like how parents talk about them on the baseball field, they should be more conscious about the way they talk about parents, even if that conversation takes place in the faculty room. If we think of parents as partners, maybe we will be more likely to empathize with them rather than criticize and complain about them.

A friend used to say that everyone has at least one person they tell a secret or complain to. Many people may have more than one, and social media certainly opens up the opportunity to complain in front of many, many people. We need to realize that when we talk negatively about someone, that person may tell a friend, and that conversation can get passed on and on to many more people in the community. Like the telephone game, what we say may get distorted as it goes from one person to the next. When all is said and done, will the words that are tied to us make us look like caring people or callous ones?

Our words matter, and whether we like it or not, when it comes to parents, our words represent our schools and even our school districts. I used to tell my students that when they went to a play on a field trip, the people attending the play didn't necessarily know what class they were from but most certainly knew the school bus that took them there. The way we behaved as a class had ramifications for our school because we represented that school when we were out in in the community. Would the way we represented the school make everyone else in the school proud? Were we behaving like good partners to our fellow classmates back at school?

In social media, leaders and teachers also represent the schools they serve. You don't leave work behind you when you log in to Facebook. Social media has changed the way we communicate. On Twitter or Facebook, people know where you work. Others can capture screenshots of things you may say and post it for the world to see, outside of your small circle of friends. Our words now spread faster than ever. And bad news travels faster. Even if you are just posting about your personal life, if you do or say something disreputable on social media, it can reflect negatively on your school. No matter who you are speaking with or what you are talking about, try to always act as a responsible partner doing and saying things that will make your coworkers, students, and school community proud. Another way to make your school proud is to actively send messages out praising what your school does well. Acting like a good school partner is another way to positively brand your school.

BRANDING YOUR SCHOOL

Branding involves the use of social media to send a message to the community and promote the school. It's important for collaborative leaders to embrace the idea of branding. Unfortunately, too many leaders don't want to use social media, which prevents them from accelerating the branding process. Joel Gagne (2012) writes that there are three key reasons why school leaders should use social media. Those reasons are communication, public relations, and branding. Communication refers to the typical communication that schools do through the use of newsletters and website. Public relations refers to the idea that schools need to direct parents and community members to positive things happening in education because there has been a great deal of negative press around public education. The last reason, branding, has become very important for schools over the last few years.

Branding your school means exactly what you think it means. Just as McDonalds, Pizza Hut, Pepsi, and thousands of other companies explicitly work to have the public associate certain characteristics and attributes to their products, so too do schools need to explicitly work to ensure that the public associates a particular characteristic to them whether that is innovation, excellence, hard work, or teamwork. Like consumer products, schools need to know how to brand themselves.

According to Tony Sinanis and Joe Sanfelippo (2014),

> Branding, which typically is a "business world" term, is exactly what our schools need today. There is so much bashing of public education in the media today, and the landscape of public education is not a pretty one, but as educators (superintendents, classroom teachers, support specialists, or lead learners of the building); we still control most of what happens in our schools. And since we control what happens in our schools, and we know that there are awesome techniques, approaches, and programs unfolding in our schools, let's spread the word; let's brand our schools; let's fuel the perceptions; and let's create our realities. (pp. 8–9)

There are some simple ways to brand your school. The key is to associate something (hashtag, mascot, phrase, color) with the school so that every time someone sees that logo or phrase they immediately think of the school (in a positive way). Create a school hashtag on Twitter such as #PESPenguins (for the Poestenkill Elementary School mascot) or #GoCrickets for a different school. Print the hashtag on all T-shirts, backpacks, notebooks, stickers, and other school merchandise. The goal here is to create a sense of community and school spirit—your brand should make people feel good about the product (in this case, the school). In addition to hashtags and merchandise, logos, websites, and social media can also contribute to bolstering a school brand.

- **Logo**—Have a contest where students create a logo for the school. Or hire a marketing company. The student contest would be a great way to show that leaders care about student voice.

- **Website**—Make sure the logo is on the school website. Please, please, please make sure the school's co-constructed Aspiration includes the word *learning* and is prominently featured on the home page of the website.
- **Social Media**—As instructional leaders, it is very important to get your schools involved in social media. Tweeting is a must! Make sure every tweet you send out includes the school hashtag. That way, anytime anyone follows the hashtag, all of the positive tweets will come up. Tweeting is easy to do after leaders get the hang of it.

If principals truly want to be collaborative leaders, they need to find innovative ways to engage the school community. Too often, engagement used to be one sided. Many families were told what they needed to know, and that "need to know" basis didn't help build any bridges between home and school. Collaborative leaders need to move away from that old model toward fostering authentic dialogue between all stakeholders in the school community, including the use of social media.

We can no longer bury our heads in the sand and ignore social media or the power of it. Frankly, too many other school leaders are on social media, and people who work in schools, and parents who send kids to the schools where principals and superintendents are not on social media notice the absence. People see the kind of authentic communication that takes place at one school and notice its absence at another.

Taking the partnership approach to relationships between schools and stakeholders is important. New curriculum or standards are being implemented and parents are at a loss as to how to help their children. High-stakes testing is at the center of a great deal of debate and as parents opt their children in to take the test, other parents are opting their children out by the thousands. This all has an enormous effect on the school community. Collaborative leaders need to focus on their core aspiration and get the message out that they are focusing on learning every day.

Through working with families and engaging them in authentic ways, whether that is through face-to-face conversations or using social media tools to flip and brand, collaborative leaders find a balance in making sure everyone feels heard. All stakeholders have to understand what that means, and they have to learn to celebrate the great conversations and work through the bad ones.

//

School Story—Engaging Families at the High School Level

by Sarah Johnson, Principal of Spooner High School

Spooner, WI

In the transition from elementary to high school, systematic shifts tend to occur that reduce the engagement of parents in their child's education. Reduction in collaborative teamwork between families and school can be attributed to many reasons in any learning community. Aside from the fact that developmentally, students begin to become more independent as they get older, it appears the system closes its doors more often to families. Instead of seeking parent volunteers in the classroom, high school classrooms keep parents out. Traditional systems engage parents once per grading term, midway through on a date set by the school, which may or may not work for all families.

It is unfortunate that the high school becomes a place where we educate students during the day and communicate with parents as an afterthought. I have often reflected this trend. Why is it that we only call when there is an academic or behavioral problem? Conversely, why are the majority of interactions from parents prompted by a complaint they have related to grading practices, teacher or coach behaviors, or lack of playing time on the court?

A very real question I have often asked myself is how I can engage parents better at the high school level. While I do not have the magic answer yet, I do employ a few strategies to increase engagement with families. Truthfully, sometimes one lands well, inciting increased flow of communication and other times, they fall flat with no acknowledgement at all. I believe the key is to continue to make the attempts to engage parents by offering opportunities to get into the building and provide the communication their teenagers withhold.

Multiple Points of Communication: Simple communications framed in a variety of ways through multiple sources provide parents with the information they need. I utilize our student management system to e-mail families, including a bimonthly online newsletter. In addition, I periodically do voice calls through that system to humanize the message. Our online presence is a key way to engage families. I post often on our Twitter page and provide information to be published on Facebook and our website. Many parents check the website for daily announcements, so we continue that practice to reach that audience.

Student-Focused Content: In my newsletters, I include images of events that occur at school with captions to explain them. Highlighted are upcoming educational events during our school day. One tool that I have recently begun using is TouchCast to create short videos of the major events that occur at school. For example, recently all first-years retreated off-site to learn about respect. I captured video and still images of the day. For an hour's work, I created a short and engaging video that allowed parents a view into the event, which augmented my preview, summary, and whatever their child chose to share with them on that day. I received more responses from parents with that video than I have with any other form of communication I have provided as an administrator.

Parent Conferences "Re"Structured: First, we schedule individual families utilizing an online scheduler. Parents are able to select an appointment thereby avoiding lines. Teachers are able to know who they will be seeing to better prepare. Also, prior to conferences, teachers are already communicating progress or concern with parents so this meeting is not their first connection.

Our remaining events for the year will be a mixture of scheduled parent–teacher conferences and edcamp-style conferences for parents where teachers lead sessions related to classroom practices and schoolwide topics.

Personal Phone Calls: Personal phone calls are a great way to build relationship credit with parents before an issue occurs. When a concern does arise, my approach is to start out the conversation in an open way, seeking assistance from the parent as a team effort. Remembering that we are advocates not adversaries is crucial in keeping parents engaged through inevitable struggle.

Giving Parents a Voice: Any opportunity we can create for parents to have their voice at the table is a win. For example, our school leadership team is looking at modifying our schedule in the upcoming year. While we are in information-gathering stages, we are involving parents in our learning activities in order to allow for their voices and perspective to be heard when we move forward in decision-making.

> When a concern does arise, my approach is to start out the conversation in an open way, seeking assistance from the parent as a team effort. Remembering that we are advocates not adversaries is crucial in keeping parents engaged.

> When a concern does arise, my approach is to start out the conversation in an open way, seeking assistance from the parent as a team effort. Remembering that we are advocates not adversaries is crucial in keeping parents engaged. (Sarah Johnson)

The ultimate goal of any administrator would be to engage all stakeholders and create a dynamic that cultivates positive engagement of all. Regardless of the learning community we serve, administrators can do this through intentional, multiple communication methods, keeping our focus on students, and investing time in the relationship between parents and school.

MEET, MODEL, & MOTIVATE

Meet

- Use the words *family engagement* rather than *parental involvement* as often as possible. This means you are meeting families where they are by being inclusive of families other than the typical mother and father nuclear family.

Model

- Treat all parents as if they are partners, regardless of how often they may come to school.
- Make sure that the pictures you send out to communicate with parents are representative of the families you have within the school. Pictures that include grandparents who are the primary caregivers, gay parents, and so forth are very important.

Motivate

- Get rid of the five-page newsletter. Make it one page and put in some teasers or "Did You Know" statements. Brand it the "One-Page Refrigerator Page." You'd be amazed at how a little branding will go a long way to getting parents to read it.
- Create a Twitter hashtag for your school. Make sure the hashtag isn't already in use. If you're the Montreal Elementary School Spartans, try #MESSpartans.
- Find alternative ways to include families into the discussions around learning, using some of the "nights" I wrote about earlier.

DISCUSSION QUESTIONS

- How do you communicate with parents?
- When it comes to changes in academics at your school, how do you communicate those changes with parents? How do teachers communicate classroom changes?
- The family dynamic has changed. How do you talk with staff about the changing family dynamics? Have you had conversations around how to support gay families or those families where grandparents are the primary caregivers?

8

What Are Your
Next Steps?

Stand up. Be a leader.

Warren Bennis

THE PLACE TO START—STRENGTHS

According to Gallup's Leadership Research (Rath & Conchie, 2008),

> In the workplace, when an organization's leadership fails to focus on individuals' strengths, the odds of an employee being engaged are a dismal 1 in 11 (9%). But when an organization's leadership focuses on the strengths of its employees, the odds soar to almost 3 in 4 (73%). (p. 2)

Grab a list of your staff members and write out the strengths of each person. The exercise will help you establish a growth mind-set and it will force you look a little deeper when you enter into classrooms for observations. You will go in with the teachers' strengths in mind rather than problems that need to be solved. I am a fan of lists because it encourages me to focus on the positive. Dig deep and try hard to find a strength for every one of your teachers, even the ones that may be difficult to work with on a daily basis. For example, I worked with one teacher who I really did respect, but we were at odds from time to time because of the way she would talk with students, staff, and parents. However, one of the things that I appreciated about her was that I could always be open and honest and never needed to pull punches. If she was rough with someone, I could address it immediately and she would walk away always trying to find a better way to communicate with people. That was her strength—ability to accept constructive criticism and the ability to resolve to improve in the future.

We know through the Gallup report that "when leaders focus on and invest in their employees' strengths, the odds of each person being engaged goes up eightfold" (Rath & Conchie, 2008, p. 2). We, as adults, often approach situations with a deficit mind-set. We look at why something won't work instead of why it might. When it comes to collaborative leadership, we need not to focus on what teachers aren't doing as much as we need to focus on what they are doing and help them achieve greater success. That is what collaborative leadership is all about. The Gallup research goes on to say, "While the best leaders are not well-rounded, the best teams are. Gallup's research found that top-performing teams have strengths in four distinct domains of leadership strength: Executing, Influencing, Relationship Building, and Strategic Thinking" (Rath & Conchie, 2008, p. 2). Collaborative leadership is about understanding that adults approach each one of those four domains in different ways. Some people take them head on, others have to work out every detail before they move on, and some people want everyone to feel good before they move on. It's important to understand that not everyone approaches a situation in the same way, and some may approach those situations using methods you never thought of before, which is the last important part of the Gallup research. Gallup (Rath & Conchie, 2008) reports that,

The most effective leaders understand their followers' needs. People follow leaders for very specific reasons. When we asked thousands of followers, they were able to describe exactly what they need from a leader with remarkable clarity: trust, compassion, stability, and hope. (p. 3)

This is difficult work. None of this will happen overnight. Please take this into consideration as you plan your next steps.

Overall, I want principals and superintendents to be collaborative leaders, and I hope I built a case for that based on John Hattie's research. It's not easy to try to make every stakeholder happy, and the reality is that leaders should never enter into a situation thinking they will be loved by everyone. The best we can ever do as collaborative leaders is aim for win-win (Covey, 1989).

Collaborators need to find the perfect balance between inspiring stakeholders to collaborate and co-constructing building- and classroom-level goals. They believe in a high level of transparency and honesty, and have a high level of performance due to the help of stakeholders who feel they have a voice in the process.

> Collaborative leaders believe in a high level of transparency and honesty, and have a high level of performance due to the help of stakeholders who feel they have a voice in the process. Collaborative leaders put everything out in the open. They expose their thinking as well as their flaws.

Collaborative leaders put everything out in the open. They expose their thinking as well as their flaws. We know that research shows that metacognitive activities enhance learning where students are concerned, and we should model that same approach using metacognitive thinking with our stakeholder groups. Collaborative leaders show that leadership is hard work while at the same time working in partnership with all stakeholders.

Leadership is not for the faint of heart. We know that whenever we move forward we are at risk of setbacks. But, as you think about your next steps understand that movement forward exposes us to the implementation dip. When experiencing the implementation dip, it is important to gather your resources and wits about you and take the necessary steps to carry on.

THE IMPLEMENTATION DIP

Whenever leaders and teachers implement something new, no matter how great it might be, there will always be an implementation dip. In fact, Michael Fullan writes that implementation dips are signs of successful schools. You cannot implement change without experiencing some setbacks, and you cannot lead a successful school without trying out innovative ideas. In *Leading in a Culture of Change* (2007), Fullan writes that

> *all* successful schools experience "implementation dips" as they move forward. . . . "The implementation dip is literally a dip in performance and confidence as one encounters an innovation that requires new skills and new understandings. (p. 40)

The key to continuing with an innovative implementation after the inevitable dip is to understand how and why the dip happened and to take steps to recover from it quickly with minimal damage. According to Fullan (2007), the dip results from two kinds of problems: (1) people react to a fear of change, and (2) the implementation is impeded by a lack of know-how regarding how to make the change work. Therefore, successful leaders need to act on two fronts at once. They have to maintain "an urgent sense of moral purpose" and continue to "measure success in terms of results," but at the same time, they need to work as motivators who inspire stakeholders to recommit to the work of implementation. Successful leaders of change need to get their staff on board and need to choose courses of action that are the most "likely to get the organization going and keep it going" (p. 41).

Regardless of how well leaders have laid the groundwork for successful implementation, the first few months are inevitably bumpy. There is always a learning curve. In *Change Leader* (2011), Fullan writes,

> Once we brought this out in the open, a lot of people immediately felt better knowing that it is normal and everyone goes through it. This finding led to the realization that we needed to focus on capacity building at this critical stage. (p. 66)

According to Fullan (2011), what separates the successful change leaders from those who are less successful is that the effective ones are able to apply a few key strategies that result in a breakthrough. An example of this would be "immense moral commitment to a cause" combined with empathy for those who are implementing the change (your staff and school community). By combining resolute commitment with empathy, successful leaders are able "to find alternative approaches when they get stuck" (p. 67).

Fullan's finding corroborates much of what has been said in this book about collaborative leadership—your initiatives will not be successful unless you solicit the support and contributions of others and inspire them to be just as committed to the work as you are.

Although the implementation dip might be inevitable, there are nonetheless steps that should be taken to ameliorate its impact as much as possible. It is incumbent upon successful school leaders to do the necessary prep work ahead of time to avoid predictable pitfalls whenever possible. As alluded to in the previous section, the prep work needs to happen on two fronts: getting your stakeholders on board and doing your homework before hand so that you are prepared with all of the knowledge and skills you need to complete the implementation.

There are at least four foreseeable obstacles that need to be considered when planning a significant change: time, understanding, resources, and people. Below is an excerpt from 4 *Obstacles to Implementation* (DeWitt, 2014e) discussing these obstacles.

- **Time**—No one can seem to find it when it has to do with something they don't want to change. We can find time to complain in the hallways, but we seem to lack time when it comes to implementation. Time and teacher voice go hand in hand. If teachers have had an opportunity to have a voice in the implementation, they will most likely be able to find the time to be a positive part of the implementation. Involve teachers in the planning stages.

- **Understanding**—Why the change? Has it been well articulated over a long period of time with data and research to back up the need? Or has it been dropped on people and they didn't see it coming? Getting people to understand the need for the implementation is key, which is why structural meetings like Principals Advisory Council or faculty meetings are such a great venue. They are especially important if teachers are actually allowed to share their thoughts and feedback. Make sure your stakeholders understand why the implementation is necessary; offer them a forum to share their thoughts and feedback. If warranted, make alterations in the plan based on the feedback. This will lead to a stronger plan with built-in support.

- **Resources**—Leaders shouldn't start the implementation if they don't have the proper resources to back up the change. It sounds silly but many changes begin before the proper resources have been purchased or utilized. Take the time to research what the best resources are, which means reaching out to other leaders and teachers in other districts . . . which takes us back to time. Do your homework. Have your ducks in a row before starting on the journey.

- **People**—Leaders know it's important to get the right people on board. This goes back to Andy Hargreaves and Dennis Shirley's focus on human capital. The problem is that the wrong people can disrupt the process even when the right people are on board. There are people in schools, both leaders and teachers, who try to sink implementation, and I'm not just talking about something like the Common Core. Naysayers are everywhere, and the reasons are plentiful, but if leaders and teachers want to move forward with an implementation, they need to make sure everyone knows why they are moving forward, and the people trying to sink it need to get out of the way. Get the right people on board.

The implementation dip is something that all collaborative leaders have to work through, which is why having a strong team of stakeholders is so important. When leaders start moving forward with next steps they must be prepared for the implementation dip that will no doubt take place. Remember that not everyone is of your same mind-set, and that's OK just as long as you can all move forward stronger.

At the Visible Learning World Conference in London in January of 2016, Hargreaves gave an engaging keynote where he said, "If we're all on the same page, no one is reading the whole book." We don't always have to be on the same page because it means we are all focusing on the same section, but we do have to make sure that we are all reading from the same book.

In addition to doing the necessary prep work and research, and to securing the support of your stakeholders, another key to successful implementation is to consult your professional learning network (PLN) to see which of your colleagues has done a similar implementation in their school and to find out what you can learn from them regarding what to avoid and how to make it successful. The section below explains steps you can take to find and strengthen your PLN.

Moving Forward by
Discovering Your PLN

When looking at next steps and understanding that the implementation dip will take place as you try to implement new strategies, it is also important to understand the benefits of a professional learning network. PLNs can be made up of individuals that help you think out situations before they occur because sometimes, the members of your PLN have been through the situations long before you ever encountered them.

One of the most important uses I have found for the multitude of technological tools that have recently become available is their ability to connect me with peers who have become my community of support (PLN) and help me to improve as a leader every day. PLNs are critically important to a leader's growth. A high-quality PLN can question us, get us to question ourselves, stretch our thinking, and be our cheerleaders when we need it the most. To me, there are three main areas where leaders can find a PLN: within their school district, in regional networks, and on social media.

Within the District

When I was a new principal, I took over for Sharon Lawrence, who became the assistant superintendent. Sharon was beloved as a principal and a role model for me. It was intimidating taking over for her. As much as I could go to her, or Jo Moccia my superintendent, about anything, I didn't want to because I needed to prove to her, and mostly myself, that I could do it alone. It was most likely flawed thinking on my part, because Sharon and I did have amazing conversation.

I did, however, have Leslie, Barb, Denis, and Laura. Leslie was the director of elementary special education; Barb, Denis, and Laura were all elementary principals. Not a day went by that we didn't pick up the phone and call each other. I guess it was our version of "phone-a-friend." Being a school leader can be lonely, especially if you were like us and did not have an assistant principal. The role is different from that of a teacher, so having trusted relationships with other principals in the district where you work is key. I would not have had half the success I did without them.

Regional Networks

In upstate New York, our school systems were made up of small districts. We had regional networks that provided professional development and compliance sessions and offered other resources. At those regional meetings, we met our fellow school leaders from other districts. There are definitely benefits to networking with school leaders outside your school district. Those colleagues can provide an outside view and offer confidentiality because they won't be running into people from central office or other buildings. They can become valued members of your PLN.

Social Media

Social media is powerful. Working with Corwin, I created the *Connected Educators Series*—a series of twenty-two, short practical books geared toward connecting educators with other educators using social media and Web 2.0 technologies. I was able to find authors for all of the books simply by tapping into my own PLN—and I had only met two of them before we began the series! My relationship with all of these authors began with Twitter and Facebook and eventually led to much deeper relationships, collaborations, and mutual professional development.

My involvement with PLNs, including leaders and teachers, also led to the creation of an edcamp in upstate New York (EdcampUNY). Prior to the edcamp, we had only met in person around three times. Since then, we have become friends and have deep conversations about education through Twitter, Facebook, and Voxer.

There are so many relationships that I have fostered through social networking. We all have deep discussions about education, have worked together to voice our concerns over

> Having a PLN is a necessary requirement to being an instructional leader because your PLN will stretch your thinking, offer an encouraging word, share resources, and help you bring out your best.

high-stakes testing, and have become friends in the process.

Having a PLN is a necessary requirement to being an instructional leader because your PLN will stretch your thinking, offer an encouraging word, share resources, and help you bring out your best. A PLN, no matter whether it's through social media, regional networks, or within the same district, can help leaders get past the implementation dip.

Don't Negotiate or Regulate as Much as You Collaborate

In the past, I have worked with all types of leaders. One really liked to negotiate. He knew what he wanted before he entered into a meeting, and then he manipulated the conversation in order to get everyone to come to (his) consensus. This leader was not bad, and he was just doing what he learned to do in his leadership training; he was tired of waiting for consensus from everyone. I couldn't help but think that it would have been better if we all had known the plan ahead of time before going into the meeting. It would have helped us feel less manipulated.

I have also worked with someone who constantly regulated her staff. She checked lesson plan books on a rotating basis and asked us to explain to her what we were doing during our prep time. One time I forgot to hand in my plans on time and ran to the top of the stairs to catch her so I could hand them in. As I apologized for my lateness, she handed them back without looking and told me she never looked at my plans anyway because mine were always fine. Why did I still have to hand them in, I thought? It was because her leadership was about regulating. I still despise that moment and it was over ten years ago. Don't do that to people, especially teachers, because it makes them feel small.

There are instructional leaders and then there are administrators. Instructional leaders are the people—men and women—who approach the principalship or superintendency differently. They are actively pursuing ways to help all stakeholders, and they do it with a balance between a servant mindset and that of an instructional coach looking for blind spots, providing equality and defending marginalized populations.

There are also administrators. Those are the people I have worked with who believe that the faculty meeting is their domain; they don't have to work in partnership with others; they are all about accountability—for others. They are the ones who run the central-office party line with parents and don't delve into showing their personality. They are most likely the ones who do not engage with students in authentic dialogue; instead they ask children where they are supposed to be if they are not in class, and focus on reactive discipline alone.

Collaborative leaders are role models for students and teachers rather than someone they fear. Collaborative leaders are the ones engaging with students, teachers, and parents. They are the leaders who make mistakes, learn from them, and don't mind putting them out there for others to see. We need more of that.

In this day and age of accountability, we need more leaders who will focus on the whole child and champion the cause of a well-rounded education for all students, including those who are marginalized. Collaborative leaders go deeper every day, and then they find ways to assess and reflect on whether what they are doing matters, instead of blindly moving forward regardless of whether stakeholders are walking with them.

So, the question is this: How do we know that collaborative leadership works? Using Hattie's research was important to me to use as a guide throughout this book. Not only do I have an enormous amount of respect for John as a person, his research is the largest ever done in education and I feel fortunate to work with him. His research offered an important basis for everything I wrote in this book. One of the things I learned from John is to "Know Thy Impact." We, as leaders, need to understand how well we are doing. Are we having an impact on learning? Are we creating relationships with students, teachers, and families that will endure through tough times and move all of our dials so that we are getting better?

As collaborative leaders, we need to know that what we do matters. When it comes to assessing school climate and gauging the success of a recent implementation or innovation surveys are a good tool to use to gather feedback to see if we're doing the right thing. It's important to have a presurvey before you start any new interventions such as flipping. See where the stakeholders are when it comes to communication or the level of professional development in the faculty meetings. If survey responses suggest that you could do a better job communicating (you could ask *how* in the survey) or that faculty meetings really don't provide any new learning opportunities to teachers, you can then begin an intervention. Not only does it show that you read, reflected, and listened to the surveys, it shows that you want to take actionable steps as well.

Over the last two years, I have had the opportunity to learn from John Hattie, Jim Knight, Russ Quaglia, and many, many others. I have an enormous amount of respect for leadership and have noticed that not all leaders are created equally. Some leaders don't care, or at least don't seem to care, what stakeholders think. Other leaders keep following the same patterns and making the same mistakes. I hope that this book has offered some suggestions on how to lead differently and where to start.

Thank you for reading.

DISCUSSION QUESTIONS

- How will you move forward?
- What is your personal goal?
- How will you co-construct goals with teachers?

Afterword

Russell Quaglia

I distinctly remember the very first day of my very first administrative role—I entered the building reminding myself how important it is to establish a collaborative and supportive environment from the get-go. I believed that if I just communicated clearly to my staff what I wanted to accomplish, we would "collaborate" and work toward achieving *my* ideas and *my* suggestions—all based on *my* values and *my* beliefs of how things should be. In reality, the only thing my definition of *collaboration* and Peter's definition have in common is the spelling! In my early administrative years, I did not work toward creating a collaborative environment built on open communication. I was a control freak who approached collaboration as a leadership technique for "doing what I wanted with the blessing of others"! While it took me a little on-the-job training to appreciate the difference, my hope for you is that after reading this book, you can start tomorrow on the right (collaborative!) foot.

Collaborative Leadership has confirmed what I have, over the years, come to realize as a core truth in education: We must create an educational learning community grounded in trust and responsibility, not testing and accountability. Today's schools are too focused on the latter. Peter has provided a framework to challenge our current thinking, make us reflect, and perhaps even become a little uncomfortable with current practices as

school leaders. It is important to recognize that the discomfort
is an opportunity for progress, a chance to truly collaborate
in a way that fosters the growth of all stakeholders. Peter has
challenged us to have higher expectations of ourselves and
those around us—to work collaboratively, simultaneously
building trust and responsibility among all stakeholders striving to reach shared goals.

Over the past thirty years, my work with student, teacher,
and principal voice has taught me that collaboration is about
more than working cooperatively—effective collaboration is
built on a foundation of listening and learning. Listening is
the key first step, and it is about more than simply hearing
someone. It requires preparation, an open mind, and a genuine interest in understanding the thoughts and ideas of those
around you. Listening needs to be more than a polite gesture;
the true value is in learning from what is heard. The successful
development of your *leader voice* hinges on the fundamental
belief that people around you have something to teach you.

Peter's model of Meet, Model, & Motivate demonstrates
the critical importance of listening and learning. He makes it
clear that collaboration is not a passive activity; it does not
spontaneously occur by wishing for it. Rather, collaboration
occurs with conscious efforts to reflect on our own behaviors,
learn from others, and lead together in a manner that is meaningful for everyone involved.

Fostering a collaborative culture is critical to success in
schools, and leaders must be mindful of the current reality
of the relationships between leadership and the staff as they
move forward. Our data from the Quaglia Institute shows
that only 48 percent of teachers today believe effective communication exists in their school. This may be surprising, yet
it is understandable when you realize that only 59 percent
feel confident voicing their honest opinion and ideas, and
only 60 percent claim that building administration is willing
to learn from staff. If leaders are to be effective collaborators,
they must first understand and be willing to listen and learn

differently—in a way that fellow stakeholders in their schools can believe in and respond to.

Being a visionary leader and a collaborator are not mutually exclusive; in fact, the latter enhances the former. Leaders who develop a vision for their school through collaboration and co-constructing of goals foster the engagement and motivation of all stakeholders. Peter clearly illustrates how each and every day leaders are faced with the challenge of determining when to negotiate, regulate, and in some cases, be a bystander. While the decision will appropriately vary to suit each situation, the underlying consistency should be a willingness to work collaboratively to ensure that the school as a whole—and everyone in it—thrives.

Our data demonstrates the significance of this:

When school leaders are perceived as being willing to listen and learn from their staff, that staff are **3x** more likely to work hard toward their goals.

When school leaders take the time to really understand and appreciate their staff, they are **6x** more likely to be creative.

When teachers have voice, they are **4x** more excited about their future in education.

As Peter has brilliantly done throughout the book, I challenge you to reflect on *who* you are as a leader and how you can work with others to make a difference. What inspires you to **meet**, listen, and learn from others? What do you do to let the people around you know that you believe in them and value their ideas and contributions? How do you let your staff know you will never be satisfied with status quo? In what concrete ways do you **model** that you are committed to working together for the benefit of all? And finally, do you **motivate** all stakeholders (including yourself!) to continuously improve?

This book incorporates the invaluable life lessons Peter has learned from being a school leader and collaborator. It also highlights how his collaboration with great educational thought leaders, such as John Hattie and Jim Knight, has contributed to the development of the Collaborative Leadership Model—a model that encourages all of us to reflect on who we are, why we are this way, and how we can improve.

Collaborative Leadership challenges us to move the dial at a time when school leaders are more concerned about surviving than thriving. Even though trust and responsibility are the most important components, the educational system is predominantly driven by testing and accountability. How do *you* break that cycle? By acknowledging the potential of the people around you and honoring their voices. By being a leader who is both visionary and collaborative—one who works with all stakeholders to make a *shared* vision a reality. We are all in this together—it is time we start leading that way.

Peter is a living example of his own Meet, Model, & Motivate construct. Thank you, Peter, for epitomizing this, and for compelling all of us to reflect on and truly understand our purpose in education. You have engaged our intellect . . . in a collaborative way!

References

AARP. (2011). *Grand facts. State fact sheets for grandparents and other relatives raising children.* American Association for Retired Persons. Retrieved from http://www.aarp.org/relationships/friends-family/grandfacts-sheets/

Armstrong, P. (n.d.). *Bloom's Taxonomy.* Retrieved from https://cft.vanderbilt.edu/guides-sub-pages/blooms-taxonomy/

Ashton, P. T., & Webb, R. B. (1986). *Making a difference: Teachers' sense of efficacy and student achievement.* New York, NY: Longman.

Ashton, P. T., Webb, R. B., & Doda, N. (1983). *A study of teacher's sense of efficacy: Final report to the National Institute of Education, executive summary.* Gainesville: University of Florida.

Bandura, A. (1997). *Self-efficacy: The exercise of control.* New York, NY: W.H. Freeman.

Biggs, J. (n.d.). *SOLO taxonomy.* Retrieved from http://www.johnbiggs.com.au/academic/solo-taxonomy/

Biggs, J., & Collis, K. (1982). *Evaluating the quality of learning: the SOLO taxonomy.* New York, NY: Academic Press.

Bloom, B. (Ed.). (1956). *Taxonomy of educational objectives: Book 1 cognitive domain.* White Plains, NY: Longman.

Bolman, L. G., & Deal, T. E. (2013). *Reframing organizations: Artistry, choice & leadership* (5th ed.) San Francisco, CA: Jossey-Bass.

Brinson, D., & Steiner, L. (2007). *Building collective efficacy: How leaders inspire teachers to achieve.* Washington, DC: The Center for Comprehensive School Reform and Improvement.

Clarke, S. (2015, May 8). Formative assessment: The right question at the right time (Web log post). *Finding Common Ground.* Retrieved from http://blogs.edweek.org/edweek/finding_common_ground/2015/05/formative_assessment_the_right_question_at_the_right_time.html

Cognition Education. (2015). *Visible learning research hub.* Retrieved from http://visiblelearningplus.com/content/visible-learning-research-hub

Cohen, J., Lopez, D., Savage, J., & Faster, D. (2015). *School climate guide for district policymakers and educational leaders.* New York, NY: National School Climate Center.

Constantino, S. (2016). *Engage every family: Five simple principles.* Thousand Oaks, CA: Corwin.

Covey, S. (1989). *The 7 habits of highly effective people.* New York, NY: Simon & Schuster.

Danielson, C. (2015, June). Framing discussions about teaching. *Educational Leadership, 72*(9), 39–41.

DeWitt, P. (2011a, October 2). Our words matter (Web log post). *Finding Common Ground.* Retrieved from http://blogs.edweek.org/edweek/finding_common_ground/2011/10/our_words_matter.html

DeWitt, P. (2011b, November 21). Why educators should join Twitter (Web log post). *Finding Common Ground.* Retrieved from http://blogs.edweek.org/edweek/finding_common_ground/2011/11/why_educators_should_join_twitter.html

DeWitt, P. (2012a, April 1). Relationships Matter (Web log post). *Finding Common Ground.* Retrieved from http://blogs.edweek.org/edweek/finding_common_ground/2012/04/relationships_matter.html

DeWitt, P. (2012b, September 2). The flipped faculty meeting (Web log post). *Finding Common Ground.* Retrieved from http://blogs.edweek.org/edweek/finding_common_ground/2012/09/the_flipped_faculty_meeting.html

DeWitt, P. (2012c, December 13). Does your school climate focus on learning? (Web log post). *Finding Common Ground.* Retrieved from http://blogs.edweek.org/edweek/finding_common_ground/2013/12/does_your_school_climate_focus_on_learning.html

DeWitt, P. (2013a, March 24). Why would anyone want to be a school leader? (Web log post). *Finding Common Ground.* Education Week. Retrieved from http://blogs.edweek.org/edweek/finding_common_ground/2013/03/why_would_anyone_want_to_be_a_school_leader.html

DeWitt, P. (2013b, July 7). Take a risk . . . Flip your parent communication (Web log post). *Finding Common Ground.* Retrieved from

http://blogs.edweek.org/edweek/finding_common_ground/
2013/07/take_a_risk_flip_your_parent_communication.html

DeWitt, P. (2013c, August 30). Why schools should care about John Hattie's visible learning (Web log post). *Finding Common Ground*. Retrieved from http://blogs.edweek.org/edweek/finding_common_ground/2013/08/why_should_schools_care_about_john_hatties_visible_learning.html

DeWitt, P. (2014a). *Flipping leadership doesn't mean reinventing the wheel* (Connected Educators Series). Thousand Oaks, CA: Corwin.

DeWitt, P. (2014b, February 28). What's our best taxonomy? Bloom's or SOLO? (Web log post). *Finding Common Ground*. Retrieved from http://blogs.edweek.org/edweek/finding_common_ground/2014/02/whats_our_best_taxonomy_blooms_or_solo.html

DeWitt, P. (2014c, April 2). High noon: The showdown over testing (Web log post). *Finding Common Ground*. Retrieved from http://blogs.edweek.org/edweek/finding_common_ground/2015/04/high_noon_the_showdown_over_high_stakes_testing.html

DeWitt, P. (2014d, November 5). 5 reasons schools need instructional coaches (Web log post). *Finding Common Ground*. Retrieved from http://blogs.edweek.org/edweek/finding_common_ground/2014/11/5_reasons_we_need_instructional_coaches.html

DeWitt, P. (2014e, November 9). 4 obstacles to implementation (Web log post). *Finding Common Ground*. Retrieved from http://blogs.edweek.org/edweek/finding_common_ground/2014/11/4_obstacles_to_implementation.html

DeWitt, P. (2015a, January 8). It's time to stop ignoring data (Web log post). *Finding Common Ground*. Retrieved from http://blogs.edweek.org/edweek/finding_common_ground/2015/01/its_time_to_stop_ignoring_data.html

DeWitt, P. (2015b, February 22). Letting parents in on the secret of school (Web log post). *Finding Common Ground*. Retrieved from http://blogs.edweek.org/edweek/finding_common_ground/2015/02/letting_parents_in_on_the_secret_of_school.html

DeWitt, P. (2015c, March 12). What if you had 5 minutes to inspire a teacher? (Web log post). *Finding Common Ground*. Retrieved from http://blogs.edweek.org/edweek/finding_common_ground/

2015/03/what_if_you_only_had_5_minutes_to_inspire_a_teacher.html

DeWitt, P. (2015d, March 24). Teacher voice: 8 Conditions that are harder than you think (Web log post). *Finding Common Ground.* Retrieved from http://blogs.edweek.org/edweek/finding_common_ground/2015/03/teacher_voice_8_conditions_that_are_harder_than_you_think.html

DeWitt, P. (2015e, March 29). Leaders: Are your teacher observations active or passive? (Web log post). *Finding Common Ground.* Retrieved from http://blogs.edweek.org/edweek/finding_common_ground/2015/03/leaders_are_your_teacher_observations_active_or_passive.html

DeWitt, P. (2015f, April 10). 3 reasons why faculty meetings are a waste of time (Web log post). *Finding Common Ground.* Retrieved from http://blogs.edweek.org/edweek/finding_common_ground/2015/04/3_reasons_why_faculty_meetings_are_a_waste_of_time.html

DeWitt, P. (2015g, October 20). John Hattie's 10th mindframe for learning (Web log post). *Finding Common Ground.* Retrieved from http://blogs.edweek.org/edweek/finding_common_ground/2015/10/hatties_10th_mindframe_for_learning.html

DeWitt, P. (2016a, January 10). Why we need to talk about evidence (Web log post). *Finding Common Ground.* Retrieved from http://blogs.edweek.org/edweek/finding_common_ground/2016/01/why_we_need_to_talk__about_evidence.html

DeWitt, P. (2016b, January 17). Why leaders should attend teacher trainings (Web log post). *Finding Common Ground.* Retrieved from http://blogs.edweek.org/edweek/finding_common_ground/2016/01/why_do_leaders_should_attend_teacher_trainings.html

DeWitt, P., & Hattie, J.A. C. (2015, November 6). Flipped leadership is collaborative leadership (Web log post). *Finding Common Ground.* Retrieved from http://blogs.edweek.org/edweek/finding_common_ground/2015/11/flipping_and_the_cycle_of_collaborative_leadership.html

DeWitt, P., & Moccia, J. (2011, May). Surviving a school closing. *Educational Leadership, 68*(8), 54–57. Alexandria, VA: ASCD.

DeWitt, P., & Slade, S. (2014). *School climate change: How do I build a positive environment for learning?* Alexandria, VA: ASCD.

Donohoo, J. (2013). *Collaborative inquiry for educators: A facilitator's guide to school improvement.* Thousand Oaks, CA: Corwin.

Donohoo, J., & Velasco, M. (2016). *The transformative power of collaborative inquiry: Realizing change in schools and classrooms.* Thousand Oaks, CA: Corwin.

Eells, R. (2011). Meta-analysis of the relationship between collective teacher efficacy and student achievement (Doctoral dissertation). *Dissertations,* Paper 133. Retrieved from http://ecommons.luc .edu/luc_diss/133

Ferriter, B. (2012, July 7). What if you flipped your faculty meetings? (Web log post). *The Tempered Radical.* Retrieved from http://blog .williamferriter.com/?s=+What+if+you+flipped+your+faculty+ meetings

Fullan, M. (2007). *Leading in a culture of change.* San Francisco, CA: Jossey-Bass.

Fullan, M. (2011). *Change leader: Learning to do what matters most.* San Francisco, CA: Jossey-Bass.

Fullan, M. (2014). *The principal: Three keys to maximizing impact.* San Francisco, CA: Jossey-Bass.

Fullan, M., & Quinn, J. (2015). *Coherence: The right drivers in action for schools, districts, and systems.* Thousand Oaks, CA: Corwin.

Gagne, J. (2012). *Why school leaders must embrace social media now.* Retrieved from http://www.forbes.com/sites/dorieclark/2012/ 08/23/why-public-school-leaders-must-embrace-social -media-now/

Goddard, R. D., Hoy, W. K., & Woolfolk Hoy, A. (2000). Collective teacher efficacy: Its meaning, measure, and impact on student achievement. *American Educational Research Journal, 37*(2), 479–507.

Hargreaves, A., & Shirley, D. (2012). *The global fourth way: The quest for educational excellence.* Thousand Oaks, CA: Corwin.

Hattie, J. A. C. (2009). *Visible learning.* London, England: Routledge.

Hattie, J. A. C. (2012a). *Visible learning for teachers: Maximizing impact on learning.* London, England: Routledge.

Hattie, J. A. C. (2012b, September). Know thy impact. *Educational Leadership,70,*18–23.

Hattie, J. A. C. (2015a). *What doesn't work in education: The politics of distraction.* London, England: Pearson.

Hattie, J. A. C. (2015b). *What works best in education: The politics of collaborative expertise.* London, England: Pearson.

Henderson, A. T., & Mapp, K. L. (2002). *A new wave of evidence: The impact of school, family, and community connections on student achievement.* Austin, TX: The National Center for Family and Community Connections with Schools.

Hook, P. (n.d.). *SOLO taxonomy versus Bloom's Taxonomy.* Retrieved from http://pamhook.com/wiki/SOLO_Taxonomy_versus_Bloom%27s_Taxonomy

James-Ward, C., Fisher, D., Frey, N., & Lapp, D. (2013). *Using data to focus instructional improvement.* Arlington, VA: ASCD.

Jeyens, W. H. (2005). *Parental involvement and student achievement: A meta-analysis.* Cambridge. MA: Harvard Family Research Project. Retrieved from http://www.hfrp.org/publications-resources/browse-our-publications/parental-involvement-and-student-achievement-a-meta-analysis

Jones, B. R. (2014). *The focus model: Systematic school improvement for all schools.* Thousand Oaks, CA: Corwin.

Knight, J. (2007). *Instructional coaching: A partnership approach to improving instruction.* Thousand Oaks, CA: Corwin.

Knight, J. (Ed.). (2008). *Coaching: Approaches & perspectives.* Thousand Oaks, CA: Corwin.

Knight, J. (2011). *Unmistakable impact: A partnership approach for dramatically improving instruction.* Thousand Oaks, CA: Corwin.

Knight, J. (2013). *High-impact instruction: A framework for great teaching.* Thousand Oaks, CA: Corwin.

Le Fevre, D. M., & Robinson, V. M. J. (2014, April). The interpersonal challenges of instructional leadership: Principals' effectiveness in conversations about performance issues. *Educational Administration Quarterly,* 1–38. doi:10.1177/0013161X13518218

Littky, D. (with Grabelle, S.). (2004). *The big picture: Education is everyone's business.* Alexandria, VA: ASCD.

Lofquist, D. (2011). *Same-sex couple households.* Washington, DC: U.S. Census Bureau.

National Parent Teacher Association. (2015). *National standards for family-school partnerships.* Retrieved from http://www.pta.org/programs/content.cfm?ItemNumber=3126

National School Climate Center. (2014). *School Climate.* Retrieved from https://schoolclimate.org/climate

Quaglia, R. J., & Corso, M. J. (2014a). *Student voice: The instrument of change*. Thousand Oaks, CA: Corwin.

Quaglia, R. J., & Corso, M. J. (2014b). Student voice: Pump it up. *Principal Leadership*. Reston, VA: National Association of Secondary School Principals.

Quaglia Institute of Student Aspirations. (2015). *Teacher voice report 2010–2014*. Thousand Oaks, CA: Corwin.

Rath, T., & Conchie, B. (2008). *Strengths based leadership: Great leaders, teams and why people follow*. New York, NY: Gallup Press.

Robinson, V. (2011). *Student-centered leadership*. San Francisco, CA: Jossey-Bass.

Robinson, V., Lloyd, Clair A., & Rowe, Kenneth J. *The Impact of Leadership on Student Outcomes: An Analysis of the Differential Effects of Leadership Types*. University of Auckland, New Zealand

Saulney, S. (2011). Census data presents rise in multiracial population of youths. *The New York Times*. Retrieved from http://www.nytimes.com/2011/03/25/us/25race.html?_r=0

Scharmer, C. O. (2003). *The blind spot of leadership: Presencing as a social technology of freedom*. Habilitation Thesis.

School Leaders Network. (2014). *Churn: The high cost of principal turnover*. Retrieved from http://connectleadsucceed.org/sites/default/files/principal_turnover_cost.pdf

Sinanis, T., & Sanfelippo, J. (2014). *The power of branding: Telling your school's story*. (Connected Educators Series). Thousand Oaks, CA: Corwin.

Sinek, S. (2009). *Start with why: How great leaders inspire everyone to take action*. New York, NY: Penguin.

Sparks, S. (2015, July 1). *Survey suggests social-emotional learning has staked a claim in schools* (Web log post). Retrieved from http://blogs.edweek.org/edweek/inside-school-research/2015/06/social_and_emotional_learning.html

Stewart, W. (2015). Leave research to the academics, John Hattie tells teachers. *TES Connect*. London, England. Retrieved from https://www.tes.com/news/school-news/breaking-news/leave-research-academics-john-hattie-tells-teachers

Teacher Voice Report - http://www.tvaic.org/docs/TeacherVoice Report.pdf

Thapa, A., Cohen, J., Higgins-D'Alessandro, A., & Guffey, S. (2012). *School climate research summary: August 2012*. New York, NY: National School Climate Center.

Timperley, H., Wilson, A., Barrar, H., & Fung, I. (2007). *Teacher professional learning and development: Best evidence synthesis iteration.* Wellington, New Zealand: Ministry of Education.

Tschannen-Moran, M., & Gareis, C. R. (2015). Principals, trust, and cultivating vibrant schools. *Societies, 5*(2), 256–276.

Welcome, A. (2014, October 12). Why your whole staff should be on Twitter. *Finding Common Ground.* Retrieved from http://blogs.edweek.org/edweek/finding_common_ground/2014/10/why_your_whole_staff_should_be_on_twitter.html

Welcome, A., Durham, K., Kloczko, J., & Saibel, E. (2014, September 7). Leaders: Get out of your office! *Finding Common Ground.* Retrieved from http://blogs.edweek.org/edweek/finding_common_ground/2014/09/Leaders_get_out_of_your_office.html

Whitaker, T. (2003). *What great principals do differently: Fifteen things that matter most.* Larchmont, NY: Eye on Education.

Wiggins, G. (2012). Seven keys to effective feedback. *Instructional Leadership, 70*(1), 10–16.

Index

A SAGE Publishing Company

CORWIN HAS ONE MISSION: to enhance education through intentional professional learning.

We build long-term relationships with our authors, educators, clients, and associations who partner with us to develop and continuously improve the best evidence-based practices that establish and support lifelong learning.

THE PROFESSIONAL LEARNING ASSOCIATION

Learning Forward is a nonprofit, international membership association of learning educators committed to one vision in K–12 education: Excellent teaching and learning every day. To realize that vision, Learning Forward pursues its mission to build the capacity of leaders to establish and sustain highly effective professional learning. Information about membership, services, and products is available from www.learningforward.org.

Solutions you want. Experts you trust.
Results you need.